Benchmarking:

In Theory

And Practice

Kenneth Stork
James P. Morgan

f

TABLE OF CONTENTS

Acknowledgements

In 1993, Jack O'Connor, publisher and vice president of Purchasing Magazine, asked me to write a monthly column for Purchasing. I pleaded that I was too busy with my year-old consulting business. But Jack cinched the deal by using on me some of my frequent advice: When you want something done, ask a busy person. Then I said, "What do you want me to write about?" Jack responded, "We'll ask Jim Morgan for his recommendations."

Jim, who recently retired as editorial director and vice president of Purchasing Magazine, came up with the novel thought that a monthly column on benchmarking might provide some value to his 100,000 or more readers. Jim volunteered his observations that benchmarking had played a significant role in the successful renewal of Motorola as a total company, and, more specifically, in the supply management process improvements I led. Motorola received much acclaim for winning in 1988, the first Malcolm Baldrige National Quality Award, and other awards, such as Purchasing's 1991 Purchasing Medal of Professional Excellence.

I agreed with Jim's benchmarking theme idea for several reasons.

First, benchmarking as a process had played a major role in helping me advance my career. I discovered I did something unusual every time I was promoted or joined a new company in a new industry. I successfully sought out the advice and counsel of older, wiser, highly successful executives in my new position. I learned many useful processes, ideas, tools, etc. I also saw what not to do, or what I call reverse benchmarks.

A recent column dwelled on the great lessons I learned in 1978, shortly after I was hired by Motorola as corporate manager of materials and purchasing management. I wish memory, time, and space allowed a proper acknowledgement of all the many contributors to my personal success.

Second, as an early pioneer of supply chain management practices and someone whose career had not started in purchasing, I had strong, constructive criticisms of conventional purchasing practices. I intuitively felt there had to be better ways and that customer-supplier relationships should not be adversarial, arm's length, contractually and transactionally oriented, etc.

I owe a profound debt to many business associates and suppliers who helped me uncover, create, and implement new relationships based on trust, mutual benefits, or win-win. I applaud people like Jim West and Steve Soto of Motorola who were willing to try out one of my wilder ideas in 1980—allowing us to provide the supplier (who should be a single source) with our entire MRP planning horizon so we could make lead times very short. Jim, Steve, and many others were the pioneers for schedule sharing which improved Motorola's inventory turns by $1.7 billion. People willing to try a new idea are so rare and special—even today.

In recent years there has been unprecedented senior management interest in supply chain management, the new frontier for major cost reductions and competitive advantage. CEOs are beginning to be concerned about competing through their supply chains—versus the competitors and their chains.

But, far too many purchasing organizations are far behind the stampede for effective supply chain management. My intent with the past monthly columns and now with this book is to share lessons learned plus observations on the benchmarking highway and to offer pragmatic, useful advice to anyone interested in accelerating the rate of improvement in their organizations. I have attempted to minimize the theory and emphasize the practice side. My primary intent is to help more people get started, and to have early successes, like I did.

I wish I could properly thank all the new associates I have teamed up with over the past seven years. Being able to to help so many customers to find better ways is a pleasure I treasure.

I owe a major debt to Jim Morgan for making this book a reality. If you like it, Jim deserves the credit.

Finally, I owe so much to my wife, Sandee, who is a true partner supporting me both professionally and personally. Sandee, and our children, Keith, Michael, Jay, and Vicki, have encouraged and supported me along risky, but rewarding new directions.

Thank you to everyone who has contributed.

Sincerely,
Ken Stork
May 1999

Preface

BENCHMARKING: IN THEORY AND PRACTICE

What it is and some insights into benchmarking's use as a competitive tool in corporate America

As never before, many firms are searching for ways to better understand how they are performing in such areas as quality, cost, product features, customer satisfaction, and technology. Many, in fact, are looking within themselves in efforts to explore what can be done to shape processes in a way that they contribute to improved performance.

At the heart of this introspection is competition. As never before global competition is driving the need to reduce the time it takes to make improvements and institutionalize the processes involved in bringing about improvement. Companies and functions within companies are seeking to establish continuous improvement and the competitive advantage and flexibility that often accompanies the continuous improvement ethic.

What drives competitiveness

Lest anyone infer from the above that global competition is driving the business world into hiding, be it known that the business scene has become more competitive than ever. What's different is that more attention is being paid directly to the processes that most affect competitiveness. Companies are taking a more rational approach to examining the competitive advantages and disadvantages of their processes and the processes of their competitors. More often than not companies are acquiring and applying good ideas from a wide array of sources.

The name of this initiative is "process benchmarking," and although many in business treat it as a new philosophy, it has been around for a number of years. What makes benchmarking so important is that it provides the logic needed to drive most of the competitive initiatives now being put in place by companies.

One of the most cited definitions of benchmarking is that it is a "continuous, systematic process for evaluating the products, services, and work processes of organizations that are recognized as representing best practices for the purpose of organizational improvement." Another often cited definition holds that benchmarking is a "continuous, systematic process used to drive change into an organization." This definition says that benchmarking arrives at change by doing process to process comparisons and developing data about performance output levels for the process. In other words, benchmarking is the "search for those practices that lead to superior performance."

The key words in both definitions are "continuous" and "systematic." In both there is an implied understanding that the process is ongoing and that the people undertaking benchmarking are doing so with a measure of understanding and knowledge. This is not a process where someone merely picks up the phone and starts dialing. Nor is it a type of polling initiative where companies or organizations compare where they are and then file the information away to be looked at in another year—or even periodically.

What it is and is not

Many of those most involved in benchmarking say that the best way to understand what benchmarking is about is to look at what it is not. For example, benchmarking is neither competitive nor comparative analysis, where the analyst looks at his or her company's products or compares his or her company to another in terms of such things as productivity rate, cost of producing a product, or quality levels. Though this type of analysis usually plays a major role in benchmarking, it is not what is meant by process benchmarking. Why? Because it typically doesn't drive change and does not focus on processes.

Nor does comparative analysis constitute process benchmarking when the firm compares other external organizations. A typical comparative analysis might look at or compare two suppliers in terms of financial condition or manufacturing capabilities. This is not benchmarking. Neither is a firm practicing benchmarking when it looks at its internal processes and makes improvements using an internal team applying a variety of techniques. For example, a firm wants to improve accounts payable, so it looks at itself and inwardly works on process steps to fix the problem it finds. These activities, while commendable, still do not add up to process benchmarking. They simply do not go far enough. Process benchmarking would require study of other internal/external locations.

Many firms, in fact, completely miss the point of benchmarking. Some run out to a company and spend half a day asking people in the organization what they do. The people in the company tell them. These would-be benchmarkers come back with one or two ideas and try to make a change. No improvement mechanism has been developed, no clear path has been pioneered for future improvement. Overall, there is not a clear plan or approach to follow.

In plain language, process benchmarking is not just a one-time effort and it is not easily accomplished. Especially it is not a three-hour "show and tell" session with another company where they tell you what they're doing and you say, "Gee what a good idea, we'll copy it." Benchmarking starts with the use of many of the analysis techniques pioneered by value added, value engineering, and supply chain management and adds to them the empirical wisdom of successful competitors in the field.

Still, having set down what benchmarking is and is not, we're not so naive as to believe that every reader of this book will adopt benchmarking as a *cause celebre*. Many will read this book much the way many of their colleagues approach benchmarking in general. They will dabble around the edges, pick up a few good ideas, but fail to install a continuous, systematic process benchmarking program. But like the proverbial chicken soup, picking up random ideas about benchmarking, comparative analysis, or continuous improvement can't hurt. Our sincerest hope for this book is that it will spark new or renewed interest in the benchmarking process.

In theory and practice

In an effort to make this book both a useful tool and a source of new ideas and insights we laid it out in two parts. **Part 1: The elements of benchmarking** looks in detail at a number of the many facets of benchmarking—with special attention to:

• Where benchmarking fits as a part of corporate competitive strategies.

• How benchmarking is being used to drive change throughout the company.

• The elements of a good benchmarking program.

• The pitfalls that benchmarkers need to avoid in order to bring about an effective benchmarking process.

• Hints and guidelines on how to get started and what to focus on in benchmarking the benchmark program.

• An analysis of some of the inertia that surrounds many benchmarking initiatives and some hints and helpful suggestions in winning broad corporate acceptance.

• Developing useful measurement tools for benchmarking.

• How successful benchmarking is evolving into a working part of many corporate competitive strategies.

• Hints on finding benchmarking partners.

Part 2: Benchmarking in practice looks at benchmarking in terms of its everyday application in companies around the the world. Where Part 1 deals mainly with the theory of benchmarking, Part 2 is a collection of thoughtful essays by Ken Stork—the nation's premier advocate of benchmarking in American industry today. Formerly Motorola's corporate director of materials and purchasing, Stork conducts a successful consulting practice that focuses on supply chain management and strategic sourcing. He also authors a monthly column on benchmarking in Purchasing Magazine, and has been an instructor in Supplier Management at California Institute of Technology since 1993.

Stork is also a board member of two manufacturing companies. In 1993 he received a lifeime achievement award from the Electronics Purchasing group of the National Association of Purchasing Management for his many contributions to the purchasing profession.

James P. Morgan
Editorial Director Emeritus
Purchasing Magazine

Chapter 1

WHY BENCHMARKING IS SO IMPORTANT

A look at how benchmarking provides the logic and best practices and proceses needed to drive major corporate competitive initiatives.

The goal of those who are most successful at benchmarking is not a mere identification of some internal differences but the understanding of what enables the best-in-class firm to compete in an ever-expanding global market. Members of benchmarking teams need to understand the obstacles that their benchmarking partners (best-in-class) also encountered and then understand the kinds of obstacles their companies are likely to encounter. Ideally, from this understanding of problems a plan to move to a new level of competitiveness is driven into the soul of the company employing benchmarking as a tool.

What's more, benchmarking is considerably more than the exercise of some general principles that are nice to follow. In fact, researchers, consultants, and practitioners all seem to agree that benchmarking efforts, when applied correctly, can achieve significant breakthrough goals and continuous improvement changes. Typically, they note, cycle time and purchase cost reductions of 15% to 40% or more have been achieved through the application of benchmarking principles. On a one-time basis, delivery improvements of 50% are realistic goals for benchmarkers.

In many ways benchmarking should provide the logic needed to drive many of the other competitive initiatives that companies employ. Benchmarking also should play a key role in developing the competitive strategies they thrive on. Above all, benchmarking is not a passive pursuit. People need to realize that just doing benchmarking is not enough. To be effective it has to cause companies that employ it to take action and set a new philosophy. In the most successful examples, senior management is actively involved in their benchmarking projects.

Six Sigma quality

Some of the flavor of this need for benchmarking to drive change comes across in Motorola Corp.'s adoption of Six Sigma (see Chapter 4, pp. 62-65) as the major goal resulting from its benchmarking project to improve product quality. At first the Six Sigma goal (roughly no more than 3.4 quality rejections per million) looked like an impossible goal to reach. But as those who were responsible for adopting the Six Sigma goal, explain it, reaching for the goal drove the entire company into making tremendous process and behavorial changes.

As they describe the move, Motorola team members set the goal and then followed it up with research, observation, measurement, and attention to detail. Reaching for the Six Sigma qualty goal involved people going through factories in Japan and all around the world and always looking at products and trying to figure out where they were on the quality chart (defects per million). Reaching for the goal, in other words, set a totally new view of quality at Motorola as well as a totally new perspective on the goal and what it means to achieve it.

The practice of benchmarking is believed to have been started in the early 1980s and Xerox often is credited with popularizing the use of the term. But benchmarking's origins are somewhat murky because the first references to it in business were mainly in reference to comparing computer systems (i.e. the speed of one processor versus the speed of another). Even today the use of the term benchmarking in its full context is somewhat colored by its early usage in the computer field. Thus, some people still tend to refer to benchmarking strictly in terms of speeds, numbers, and ratios.

Another school of thought suggests that GE started the idea of benchmarking with its use of the term "baselining" to compare itself to other companies. In truth, the idea of baselining probably goes back several decades earlier than that. GE, it appears, was touching some of the techniques of comparative analysis when it developed value analysis around World War II.

In many ways benchmarking is seen to take the analysis in value analysis one step further. It bounces ideas off other people and organizations that are doing the same or comparable things. Benchmarking also closely resembles value analysis in the way it looks at function.

Perhaps the best explanation is that benchmarking has a number of antecedents. Lightening didn't just strike one day. The elements of benchmarking, it appears, were developed out of old wisdom and modified to fit new realities of industrial competitiveness.

Japan's early benchmarkers

Despite differences of opinion on benchmarking's origins, there is little doubt that the Japanese were among the very earliest benchmarkers and champions of what we now regard as the benchmarking process. In the years after World War II many Japanese companies appeared to be systematically soaking up the innermost secrets of the most successful American businesses. Many of the

Japanese benchmarkers added tremendous momentum to the growth of their industries by driving home the power of benchmarking as a process. In many cases they learned from the Americans by identifying the key factors in the Americans' success and then adopting and adapting them to their own specific needs and capabilities. Most important, they acquired and modified good ideas in a systematic, continuous process.

One famous story about how the Japanese identified and applied the Americans' keys to success is told about a visit by Toyota executives to the Ford headquarters in the early '80s. As the story goes, top Ford executives were extolling their Tokyo visitors for the incredible accomplishments of their Toyota Production System (TPS) and especially their implementation of what Americans came to call just-in-time manufacturing. The Japanese executives, meanwhile, assumed quizzical expressions on their faces as they looked out the window toward Ford's huge River Rouge plant in the distance.

One member of the visiting team finally said, "I really don't know why you honor us, because we learned to achieve all the successes that you celebrate, right here. This is where we learned. True, later on we brought some refinements and improvements to what you taught us. But all the original concepts were here."

As the Japanese saw it, they were using common sense and following good business practice in learning from somebody else. Meanwhile, Ford, which created the River Rouge, was moving in the opposite direction. Early in the century it had developed a thought-out moving assembly line, and for all intents and purposes Ford was doing supply chain management decades before its competitors. But by the late '70s it was in danger of being squeezed out of the auto market. It appeared to be almost unwilling to change its mode of competing to match the new realities of the marketplace.

In any case, Ford appears (for a time at least) to have fallen victum to one of the most subtle dangers in benchmarking. It became the benchmark and did what so many companies do when they are hailed for their successes—they began to believe their press clipping. When companies and organizations get into this mode they stop studying what their competitors are doing. This is usually followed by a slowdown in the rate of innovation and competitiveness. And as the benchmarked companies slow down others are learning to run faster and pass them by. In the same vein, the Japanese may have become too successful, and industries such as banking and real estate would benefit greatly by emulating America again.

Why benchmarking is so important—now

Moving from history to the present, the most significant force behind the benchmarking movement is competition. Business is changing so fast and is becoming so global that firms have less and less time to try out new things on their own. The pace of change has become so frenzied that if a company is not at the leading edge, it is almost forced to do some benchmarking to try to quickly close the gap.

More specifically, much of the current interest in benchmarking is falling in the supply management area. Senior executives in many companies have come to believe that there are vast pools of untapped opportunities in supply management—if only they put the right people and systems in place to identify them and take action.

In today's business world, if you are a manager in supply/purchasing you are or very soon will be the center of an incredible focus of attention. Incredible expectations are being built up at a senior management level. Those who can demonstrate that they can deliver on those expectations have top management's attention as never before. For those who can't, the reverse is probably true and their jobs may be jeopardy.

Those who are titularly in charge of the supply chain process and can't show significant improvement in performance of the chain almost certainly will be replaced. Supply and purchasing are no longer the comfortable places they once were. Cries that the function "gets no respect" are being put under a great deal of scrutiny. For many companies reengineering and other tools of change are calling into question what is being done in the name of performing the supply management function. A growing number of companies are no longer willing to pay even modest salaries for someone who is fundamentally a transaction processor.

At many companies where the current pace of restructuring appears to be slowing, the sense of relief is probably premature. Many companies are only in the digesting stage of their first round of change. In truth, a large number of departments are still performing only slightly modified forms of basic transaction processing. So far, much of the downsizing that has taken place has merely gotten rid of the obvious, patently outrageous forms of waste. In the next round of restructuring much more will be done to reduce the functional drag on competitiveness.

Ironically in many companies much that purchasing/supply should be involved in isn't even being touched. Many aren't even remotely beginning to deal with the problems. In many of these companies, top management is just beginning to think about "how effectively those dollars are being spent." As they begin to develop a clearer picture, the whole supply management process as it's being run will be under serious scrutiny.

Helping to push this reawakening of interest is the fact that a growing number of senior managers are taking management courses that focus on supply chain management. They are asking questions never asked before, and they are asking questions that require answers with a scope that demands more than neat homilies about right place, time, quantity, price, etc.

The driving philosophy behind benchmarking is the need to come out of the examination of a process with some sort of analysis that identifies areas of opportunity for self improvement. This is a practical philosophical approach that targets the collection of usable ideas that can be of economic benefit. Above all, it avoids a focus that is intent on classifying one company in relation to others in the field.

"We're above average" findings offer few practical benefits. The focus really needs to be on finding a few priority items that can benefit an operation. It can't be emphasized too much that benchmarking is a process where you get useful ideas and economic benefit. The better you fit the collection of ideas into a systematic, continuous process, the more you will derive from benchmarking. Our experience has been that purchasing managers have historically been lax in their use of process benchmarking as a means of creating significant, continuous improvement.

Chapter 2

A TOOL FOR DRIVING CHANGE

How this analysis tool uniquely combines performance metrics with best practices to bring about significant change.

While benchmarking provides much of the logic needed for breakthrough process changes, it is considerably more than a logic. Above all, it's a tool for driving change. This fact is readily apparent in a growing number of companies—especially where senior management is targeting supply management for competitive analysis, reverse engineering, and/or benchmarking.

In very general terms the three analytical tools stack up this way:

• Reverse engineering is generally used to compare similar products and focuses on product characteristics and functions. It is used mainly in comparing similar products.

• Competitive analysis is generally applied to market, product functions, and services and focuses on competitive strategies and tactics. It is used to influence business decisions.

• Benchmarking is applied to products, processes, and functions. It focuses on best practices and methods with the goal of developing changes leading to improved customer satisfaction.

Another term, continuous comparison, is a combination of the

THREE ANALYTICAL TOOLS (a comparison)			
Elements	**Reverse Engineering**	**Competitive Analysis**	**Benchmarking**
Purpose	Comparison to similar products	Influence business decisions	Changes leading to improved customer satisfaction
Focus	Product characteristics & functionality	Competitive strategies & tactics	Best practices, and methods
Application	Mainly manufacturing products	Market, product functions and services	Products, process and functions
Information sources	Competitors	Competitors & industry analysis	Best-in-class world-wide leaders and competitors

three and is often used to track analysis findings over periods of time.

Benchmarking where it counts

Of the three tools, benchmarking is proving to be uniquely suited to deal with inventory, purchased cost, overhead cost, and a number of other issues that are drivng supply management up earlier into the value chain. In the wake of growing competitive challenges, those in supply management are taking a very open attitude toward benchmarking and the philosophy that drives it.

Take an efficiency process—such as purchase order processing or accounts payable processing. Or take an effectiveness kind of process such as one used to incorporate suppliers' early design ideas into a product. In any of these situations, benchmarking can provide a process-to-process comparison—your firm against the best in the industry and/or the best in class on a worldwide basis.

More important though, benchmarking is primarily a tool for change. As such, it offers the most benefits compared to other analysis techniques because both performance metrics and best practices are combined with an effort to bring about real change. Performance levels are measured at specific points in time for particular process areas, e.g. purchased item ordering for inventory. Here's how performance metrics and best practices are combined in a typical benchmarking situation:

The performance benchmark involves the time it takes the company (using supplier participation) to introduce a new product. In all likelihood there already is a conventional or historic standard or metric in the industry. Let's say in this case it's 12 months.

The benchmarker now begins looking for ways to change the process to bring this down. Further study shows that a more realistic standard for new product introduction is only half the anecdotal standard. At this point the benchmarker might next look at how long it takes for firms in his or her industry and firms in other industries to perform product introduction.

Or the study might start with the firms that introduce products in the shortest possible time frame. Let's say that it's three months. Benchmarkers would then examine the processes and strategies that provided the three month introduction and learn what is being done and how the lessons learned could be applied at the firm doing the benchmarking.

A typical process benchmarking model for the above case might look like this:

• Determine what should be benchmarked based on critical

competitive forces. What in your business actually determines competitive advantage?

• Determine the companies with which the benchmarking will take place. What companies or organizations have the most valuable insights for application in your firm?

• Analyze processes and determine gaps in performance—your company and the benchmark companies.

• Establish the cause of the gap. What specific factors are responsible for the gap and is it possible to address the divergence?

• Establish the best practices to close the gap and apply—being aware that considerable modification may be needed.

Organizations leading the benchmarking movement are committing resources (dollars, people, time) to constantly learn and relearn how they can improve and stay at the leading edge in terms of competitiveness. For them it's not a one-time shot, it's competitive survival.

Part of this process benchmarking effort has to involve development of the strategies to drive change into the business. What is benchmarked is directly related to what firms need to compete in a particular product line. So companies have to be selective in what they benchmark. They need to understand which processes are most critical and what can make the biggest contribution to end results and then focus resources selectively into particular areas.

Companies also need to take the notion of benchmarking and drive it into their suppliers. One of the questions a firm might ask of its supply base is have they done a competitive analysis to understand how they measure up against competitors and can they provide evidence of whether they're best in class? This could conceivably be followed by another question: Do they have a systematic benchmarking effort that will drive them to understand levels of excellence as my long term supplier?

It also is important that benchmarking is not some instant pudding approach that leads to excellence. Firms must have a culture that allows change and breakthrough thinking. It is far too easy to be in denial and reject great useful ideas because "our business is different."

Many long-time benchmarkers also warn against trying to do too much too soon. If, for instance, your firm is beginning total quality management and process benchmarking efforts, don't try to copy immediately what the leading world class firms are doing. At an early stage your firm is probably not fully prepared to implement the full power of these approaches to drive bottom line results.

Ask the right questions

One of the big misunderstandings in applying benchmarking principles is fuzziness on the part of those applying them. To many it still boils down to some sort of sophisticated measuring. To a degree they're right. Measurement is an important part of benchmarking. But it's also an accepted truth that measurements often merely tell us what we want them to tell us or they reflect our prejudices. In short, the way we ask questions very often influences the answers we get in return. For most benchmarkers learning how to ask the right questions—asking "How?" and "Why?" enough times until problems are clear—takes precedence over development of the proper metrics.

A good example of this need to ask the right questions was demonstrated some years back during the reengineering of Ford Motor Co.'s accounts payable processes. At the time, Ford accounts payable in North America employed more than 500 people and the company was in the process of setting up a targeted headcount reduction using improved processes and systems.

ASKING WHY? AS PART OF THE
PROBLEM SOLVING PROCESS

- Why did we miss shipments last week?
- Why was production under plan?
- Why was Machine 102 down?
- Why did its' main bearing fail?
- Why didn't oil reach the bearing?
- Why was the strainer plugged?
- Who is responsible for failing to complete preventative maintenance on Machine 102 as planned?
- What will be done to prevent a recurrence?

But where to start? Several members on the reengineering team suggested benchmarking to the person in charge of the reengineering team. "Okay, he agreed," but who should we benchmark? One subordinate suggested Mazda. His reasoning: "We own about a third of the company, so if our CFO calls they gotta tell us the truth."

At the first meeting with Mazda, however, it suddenly became apparent just how hard it sometimes can be to ask meaningful questions. When asked about the size of its accounts payable department, Mazda's answer was five. "Wait," said the head of the benchmarking team. "You apparently don't understand what I mean about the accounts payable process. Currently we've got 500 people in the accounts payable department. And the invoice comes in and..."

At this point he was interrupted by one of the Mazda benchmarkers, "We don't have invoices at Mazda..."

"Let me finish," said the Ford benchmarker. "We use 500 people to take the invoices and provide a three-way match with the invoice, the receiver, and the purchase order..."

"I Hate to tell you," said the Mazda benchmarker, "but we don't have purchase orders either."

"So do you pay your suppliers?" asked the Ford benchmarker.

"Yes."

"How do you do it without invoices or purchase orders?"

"I look out the window and count how many cars we made today. Obviously we got the parts because we made the cars, so we owe our suppliers the money."

The point of the story is that benchmarking is really supposed to prompt people to get out of the mentality of ratios and ask, "Is there a totally better process for accomplishing the objective?" In answering the question it's necessary to understand that the objective is to pay suppliers, not having 500 people doing a three-way match. This kind of analytical thinking is similar to that employed by many engineering and purchasing professionals in the name of value engineering/value analysis, reverse engineering, and reengineering.

You grow into it!

How do companies move from functional evaluation to actual benchmarking? Answer: For many it's a relatively long process. There are, of course a few—very few—highly competitive companies that have been active in intelligence gathering and benchmarking over a long period of time.

But typically many companies stumble into benchmarking via relatively low-level intelligence gathering. They collect intelligence on competitors over long periods of time with no definitive objectives—or much in the way of a budget to implement them. They collect information into computer databanks waiting for a good time to use the information.

Finally, one day someone says, "Gee XYZ Co. appears to be doing some smart things in reducing the costs of transaction processing. What do we have in the file?" He wants to be the catalyst to drive XYZ's approach to paperless requisitioning into his company. He gets his information and suddenly the language of dollars comes into play and someone says "Hey boss we picked these nifty ideas out of our files on XYZ. Here's the economic value we got from these. We ought to do more of this and spread it through more of the organization."

Gradually the intelligence gathering blossoms into a full-blown benchmarking program where good ideas are systematically gathered and fit into comprehensive strategies.

Chapter 3

WHAT MAKES GOOD BENCHMARKING

The critical factors in bringing about a successful benchmarking initiative.

Benchmarking is essentially a four-step process consisting of planning, analysis, integration, and action. How well it will be done is affected by how well answers are provided at each of the four steps or phases. For instance, a good plan for continuous comparison should answer these questions:

- Who does the benchmarking?
- What will be benchmarked?
- Who will be benchmarked?
- How will the data be collected?.

The analysis step seeks to answer six basic questions:

- Does the benchmarked company outperform us?
- If so, how much better are they?
- Why is their performance better?
- What can we learn from them?
- How can we apply what we have learned?
- If our performance is better in some respects, how can we stay ahead or widen our lead?

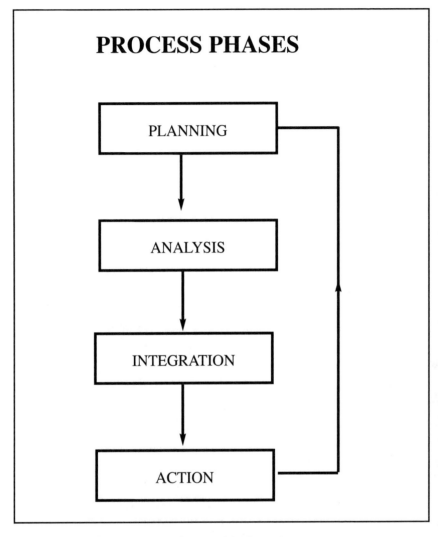

PROCESS PHASES

PLANNING

ANALYSIS

INTEGRATION

ACTION

The integration stage deals with these issues:

• Has or will management accept or buy-in to our findings and recommendations?

• Is there a need to change or modify goals and objectives?

• Have new goals been clearly communicated (or will they be

communicated) to all organizations involved? This also entails developing appropriate strategies and new operating plans and goals.

The action phase is relatively straight-forward. In it answers are sought to these three basic questions:

• Have work steps been identified to achieve our goals?

• Is progress being tracked?

• Is there a plan for recalibration—to determine if our rate of change is still appropriate?

But taking on a major benchmarking program requires considerably more than conformance to some sort of plan of attack. In fact, behind every successful benchmarking program there must be a solid foundation built on three critical success factors—commitment from top management, a thorough understanding of internal processes, and a willingness to adapt.

High level commitment

There is no equivocating about the need for commitment by top management. It has to be made aware that there is a need for change— that the company is not at the top of its game, that there are weaknesses that need to be addressed. But this recognition of a need for change has to be more than a vague recognition that something needs to be done. Somewhere in the upper levels of management there needs to be advocates and mentors of benchmarking.

These mentors in high places need to be willing and able to assure that resources will be allocated to the project in sufficient amounts to assure long term success. Along with commitment to funding, top management support will be needed to bring about substantial changes in the way processes are designed and integrated into the corporate strategy. Actually, support is the very least that's needed from top management. Real corporate commitment to benchmarking will come only when top management begins to act as a champion.

One source of optimism for the reality of this kind of change is the growing use by top management of outside assessment studies. Many top managers have come to look on them as valuable tools in building management understanding. The most popular of outside assessments are functional evaluations.

Functional evaluations of procurement are especially popular with top managers. That's because more and more top managers have come to realize in recent years that the purchasing/supply function spends a lot of the company's money (roughly 55%) and they want to see how effectively it's spent. Many use assessment by outside evaluators in building a business case for instituting needed change. Such evaluations, while they are not a substitute for a good benchmarking program, often provide a useful one-time temperature check and some suggestions for closing glaring performance gaps.

Unfortunately, there's no denying that recent good times have not been the ideal setting for attracting executive management support for benchmarking. Busy CEOs and their top executive managers often are tempted to slacken their benchmarking zeal in prosperous times.

Busy or not, executive management is sorely needed to champion the cause of benchmarking. At the very least CEOs and executive managers must be willing to do more than lend lip service to the cause of benchmarking. They need to make commitments to benchmarking, they need to throw their offices behind such commitments, and they need to do it on a long-term basis.

Furthermore, this commitment has be be made on the basis of real analysis. Corporate level executives can't afford not to use well trained, professional people to do the in-depth analysis required for a successful benchmarking project. They also have to take responsibility for ensuring that the best people are chosen to work on benchmarking projects and for the training that accompanies selection of the right people.

And executive managers' responsibilities don't end with the start of benchmarking programs. They need to learn to ask the kinds of questions that help them evaluate the relevance of the project, the fitness of those leading it, and the progress of the program and those leading it.

At the beginning and periodically during the course of the benchmarking project, executive managers need to determine whether the project organization is appropriate for goals of the project. Project structures that operate along hierarchial lines run the danger of being too inhibited to ask the kinds of questions that are needed to make benchmarking work.

Finally, in a growing number of companies, corporate executive officers are being called on to play an expanding role in driving an understanding of benchmarking throughout their companies.

Understanding the process

In arriving at an understanding of their own processes, many firms tend to confuse functions and processes. Typically those in charge tinker with the squares in the organizational box, but fail to realize that benchmarking often has to follow processes across functional lines.

For example, procurement was a function that traditionally was done totally within the confines of the purchasing department. But as management tries to apply the principles of benchmarking it often comes to realize that procurement is part of the larger process of bringing materials, supplies, equipment, and services into the company. What's more, this process crosses many organizational boundaries and involves more than the procurement department. The end user, the production scheduler, transportation, design, finance, quality control may also be involved to greater or lesser extent in this process. In fact, as their understanding grows, they start to realize that the process of feeding and managing the supply chain can fall outside of traditional organizational boundaries as well as natural reporting lines of authority. In many companies, large segments of procurement are committed and managed outside of the procurement department. Everyone fancies himself or herself as a buyer!

It's also important to understand that good benchmarking implementation depends on much more than simple process improvement. Certaintly, process improvement has to drive results, but much more is involved here. At the center of any successful benchmark study is an attempt to define the processes that are essential to competing and/or improving critical performance. These critical processes must be compared and analyzed against the processes of other best-in-class firms on a worldwide basis. From such an analysis it should be possible to determine the cause of performance gaps and eventually develop approaches to correct weaknesses and to drive performance improvement.

To really be involved in benchmarking is to understand that it is a systematic effort that will involve a number of people on a team and will take considerable time and effort. Along with requiring considerable executive commitment, the benchmarking project will require a very agile implementation team. Individual members of the team will need to recognize that they must focus on developing new information and ways of learning from others. To do this will require excellent conceptual and execution capabilities and patience to go out and analyze data.

But before the team can go out and collect data, it needs to understand the benchmarking process. Members of the team must ask themselves what they are really going to benchmark and why. They have to be ready to internally analyze their own firm so they can better compare it and share information with benchmarking partners. They have to develop focused, salient questions and provide sufficient time to get answers and further probe responses to their questions. In essence, the team needs appropriate education and training in process benchmarking.

Moreover, they need to begin to understand more about the best in the world. They have to be sure they know who the best in the world are and have the resources at a detailed level to understand how and why the best in the world do what they are doing in different process areas critical to the firm's success. They also need an attractive bait for gaining entry to conduct discussions with the best in the world.

If they follow a whole value chain of a product—from concept, to design and development, to prototyping, to service, to reclamation—along that value chain, they need to look for the leverage points. They need to locate the processes that either are costing them money or eliminating their ability to improve the end results to the customer—in terms of cycle time, cost, quality, responsiveness, delivery, etc. This form of competitive analysis begins to indicate to the firm where strategic and tactical benchmarking should be focused.

The team needs to begin to identify the key processes that are at work—that need to be understood, benchmarked, and improved in order to make the end product more competitive in the marketplace. Among the critical companywide processes that frequently yield vast improvements as the result of concentrated benchmarking efforts are order fulfillment, new product development, manufacturing setup, design change management, and customer/supplier electronic interfaces. Critical supply management processes for benchmarking analysis include supplier assessment, early supplier involvement and selection, supplier selection and sourcing, supplier development processes, accounts payable/purchasing interfaces, purchasing ordering systems and electronic commerce, purchase item inventory control and management, and internal purchasing approval processes.

Willingness to adapt

Adapting to a new way of doing things is a tough reality for many companies, but sooner or later all companies have to concede that they can't do everyting. And to make benchmarking really work, companies and organizations have to approach their commitment to benchmarking in the spirit that other people, other companies have good ideas that can be adapted to their own organizations. Unfortunately, it is all too easy to find a flaw or two in someone else's otherwise excellent approach, and subsequently reject the entire approach.

But being willing to adapt involves more that good will. The team doing the benchmarking has to recognize that when it understands its own processes and begins to look at what benchmarking partners are doing it can identify gaps between its own and best-in-class practices. In adapting to a new way of looking at and doing things, members of the benchmarking team also must be able to identify where the companies differ in both performance metrics and practices. One company, for instance, might take twice as many people as another to accomplish a task. It's up to the team members then to see if the gap is the result of multiple tasks being performed, inefficiencies, or a combination of both. It is possible that the "other" people are in strategic, high value added roles and that more resources is good, not bad, when you analyze paybacks on these resources.

Benchmarking teams also must recognize the difficulties in transferring what they see. It's a simple fact of life that the team doing the visiting usually doesn't know enough about its own processes. Typically, it comes back and says, "We have a great idea. Do this..." (ignoring the practicalities of enablers, obstacles, and implementation). Looked at on a systematic basis, benchmarking is a process in itself and takes time, effort, talented people, resourses, and management commitment.

Selection of the person who will head up the benchmarking project is one of the most critical factors. Heading the benchmarking team is a critical job and can't be spun off to the juniors on the staff. Senior people need to do much of this themselves, because the good ideas that come back from the benchmarking team need to be sold by some one with a great deal of credibility. Many times a department head will come back from a visit with several great ideas that he/she previously rejected or didn't fully embrace.

An important factor in selecting the person who will head up the benchmarking project is ability to network. People who are really good at benchmarking also have a flair for networking. In fact, if you look at it critically, benchmarking can be seen as a more organized version of networking used to accomplish specific aims in terms of a particular project that someone wants to gather information on.

"Trivial" essentials

Looking beyond the very basic requisites for benchmarking success, in the real world of implementing a benchmarking program there are a handful of essentials that look trivial, but are truly critical.

The most important of these "trivial" essentials is the need for a meaningful and doable project. In essence, when a benchmarking team starts searching out an appropriate project it needs to look for something that is focused and that the benchmarkers can get their arms around. For companies first starting out in benchmarking it's especially important that the first project is highly focused. It's ridiculous to say, "We will do a benchmarking study on supply chain management." It's simply too broad.

A more practical approach is to say, "let's take a piece of it. Dell looks pretty good, they carry only 192 hours of inventory at any time. Let's understand their planning system and how they relate to suppliers so they are able to achieve that. What are they doing differently? How do they build to demand? What are the systems they use? How is it possible to communicate to suppliers what's needed when you have a broad product mix and are not just building a few standard models? And then you have to work out how somebody else does it. And you ask yourself, "What are they doing differently? What seems to be the critical success factor that they have and we don't?"

At the end of a benchmarking visit it might be fruitful to develop answers to a more detailed list of questions that goes something like this:

• What kind of information systems do they have? Would we need to make major changes in our information systems to use their ideas?

• How do the supply people relate to the production planning people?

• What does the order fulfillment structure look like? It obviously requires more than the adoption of a classical MRP system that pushes material through the system—but what?

• What is the word from suppliers? What do they see as the good and bad points in the system?

• What are the lessons we learned about Dell's system and what do we need to do the next time we benchmark?

Setting a baseline

A second very important one of these "trivial" essentials for effective implementation is the need to set a baseline—one that identifies where you are. This is critical to developing a meaningful analysis. Say you're working on a supplier quality project, you should be able to get some meaningful answers to such questions as:

• What kind of supplier support system do we have?

• What kind of support level do we have from suppliers?

• What does their on-time delivery look like?

• What does parts per million quality look like? Is there somebody who is better or worse?

• What commodities cause the most pain?

• What performance improvement plans are in use?

The next essential is development of a survey questionnaire. You want to develop questions around things that need to be done, the practicalities of proposed projects, the weak spots that definitly have to be tackled.

In a multi-operation company the need will be to track differences from operation to operation. All good ideas don't need to start at the home operation. Branches may have the best ideas. There often are tremendous differences across divisions of large companies, and frequently no one has bothered to analyze them for ideas that can be applied in other parts of the organization.

As the other essentials begin to fall into place, the person in charge of the benchmarking project needs to start looking at specifics. He or she will want to start asking "Who's good at this?" and looking for a very focused project. Or the person in charge may need to ask, "How does this supplier handle this situation? Maybe we approach them through an e-mail..."

In any case, sooner or later the project manager starts contacting potential benchmarking partners, pointing out in words similar

---

SUCCESS FACTORS

Commitment from the top

- Need for a change
- Allocation of resources
- Integrated planning process

Understanding of your own processes

Willingness to adapt

- Can't be the best in everything
- Learning from others

---

to these, "We're working on this kind of project. Here is a list of prospective participants. If you agree to participate we will share with you an executive summary of our findings." Actually, just promising to share some findings is probably too weak. Queries to potential benchmarking partners really need to spell out in some detail what's in it for the prospective participant. You must be able to sell them on the benefits they can gain by participating. This is apt to be crucial to the success of your project. Don't blow the opportunity to build a network of relationships in best-in-class companies by allowing a lower level of employee to make an amateurish invitation.

Chapter 4

BENCHMARKING IN ACTION

A reflection on some of the barriers and enablers that seem to accompany the most acive, successful benchmarking projects.

For many of those who are the most active and successful in benchmarking, the real value of the activity comes in small pieces. There are very few processes or systems, or approaches to problems that can be transferred directly from one company to another and benchmarking is no exception. Rather, the benefits of benchmarking come from its use as generator of ideas—small ones as well as large ones. Often benchmarking teams come back from their benchmarking trips with jumbles of overlapping ideas. And as the ideas are sorted out and thought about it becomes apparent that their applicability is different from what was first imagined.

As many benchmarkers see it the value of benchmarking lies in viewing an idea, often from a nonrelated function, and recognizing how it might be put to work in another business, operation, or on a totally different problem. Many actually revel in being able to take a piece of one thing and a piece of another and blend them together to meet a totally different need or problem.

"Realistically, no one that I know has the right total system or process," says one benchmarker. "To me the analogy is a trip with friends to a Chinese restaurant. Six people enter the restaurant and each is ordering different dishes. During the meal a great deal of mixing, matching, and sampling takes place among the diners and the result is that each comes out of the restaurant having enjoyed an excellent meal and very satisfied. No one has enjoyed exactly the same meal and it doesn't matter. The diners, like good benchmarkers, are always finding another condiment or side dish to improve the next meal.

At the center of this point of view is perhaps the most important point that can be driven home by a book like this: Benchmarking is first and foremost what you make it. Learning a few things about technique may help somewhat in collecting information or getting along with people, but if that's all that results, the benchmarking project will hardly be worth the time and effort. For that reason it's necessary to examine benchmarking from the standpoint of the mindset of those practicing it and how some very successful benchmarkers just seem to arrive at success instinctively.

Actually, the most successful benchmarkers usually have a very good handle on the fundamentals. Those most successful at harnessing the benchmarking tool are often best identified by their serious and sensible approach to relationships. For example, the most successful benchmarkers can often be identified by

• How seriously they treat benchmarking.

• Their development of appropriate mechanisms for transferring information.

• Their clear appreciation of the difference between competitive analysis and benchmarking.

• Their ability to think benchmarking on more than one level.

• The humility with which they approach learning from others.

• Their good sense of timing.

• Their ability to relate benchmarking to specific corporate needs.

• Their recognition of the absolute need to have people with the ability to change things on their benchmarking teams.

• Their attention to building on prior knowledge and acquaintenances

It's for real

One thing most notable about active, successful benchmarking programs is that success is almost universally proportional to the seriousness with which benchmarking is regarded. For example, in the tale about the Toyota benchmarkers (pages 24 and 25), it's not happenstance that the teams sent to benchmark in the U.S. were sent there by their top management and given specific areas to investigate. One very remarkable factor to note about the Japanese benchmarkers is that they were among Toyota's elite. And it didn't bother the members of this select group a bit that they could learn from the River Rouge.

The easy answer for the Toyota benchmarkers would have been to say, "we don't have any of these resources the way the Americans do. We don't have integrated steel mills. We don't make tires." Instead the Japanese benchmarkers approached the trip from the standpoint of "how do we take our strengths and evaluate their strengths against the products we make? Does this analytical comparison result in a new set of principles that we operate against?"

Even with all the differences between U.S. and Japanese business in the post World War II era, the Toyota benchmarkers were able to develop useful baselines and ratios. Typically, thinking went something like this: "It takes us so many hours to build a car, and so many people, and even though Ford puts out 50 versions,

---

WHY THE JAPANESE WERE SO SUCCESSFUL

1. They came with specific understanding of the goals and objectives of their management.

2. They sent their best people.

3. They had a plan: Specific questions to ask, data to be gathered, etc.

4. They knew their status to their specific questions being asked. When better performance was found they could focus more deeply to understand the causes of the superior performance noted.

5. They had a bias for action. Knowledge/process/ practices were re-used.

6. They studied other industries for best practices. American supermarkets were the inspiration for quick replenishment/JIT/ Kanban.

7. Their process was continuous—not just a program of visits.

8. They continuously refined their process in a mode of continuous improvement.

---

we still can develop some reference points and say this is the baseline." The important part of a baseline is people always need to know where they are before they start benchmarking. They need to recognize whether someone is better or worse than themselves.

Knowledge transfer

Another truth that becomes evident from reflection on the successes of active benchmarkers is the difficulty that most benchmarkers have in transferring what they see. It's almost a truism that the team doing the visiting often doesn't know enough about its own processes. All too often the team comes back and says, "We have a great idea. Do this" ... ignoring the practicalities of enablers, obstacles, and implementation. Looked at on a systematic basis, benchmarking is a process in itself and takes time, effort, talented people, resources, and management commitment.

Typically, the benchmarking process and effort is capable of generating a wider range of options to improve processes and capabilities than is available with any other approaches.

Unfortunately, there often isn't an automatic transference of knowledge. That's why many of the most successful benchmarkers are ones who have developed systematic methodologies for driving change. Many, in fact, follow a mindset that constructs an understanding of the obstacles and the enablers to help them fix the problems as they go along. More important, many of the most successful benchmarkers build transformation and implementation plans for their organizations as they go along—based on the benchmark data and its analysis.

Benchmarking vs. competitive analysis

One area of some confusion for some benchmarkers involves sorting out the place of competitive analysis. Even though it is generally understood that competitive analysis is not process benchmarking, some degree of competitive analysis usually is needed to establish what is required to win more customers. Competitive analysis also helps establish some priorities in the benchmarking effort. If the team wants to drive quality, it needs to benchmark quality. If it wants to drive cost, it really needs to examine how it can improve the total cost and not just purchase price. If it wants to drive inventory and asset investment in a downward direction, it has to understand the processes of best-in-class firms.

Many of the most successful benchmarkers benchmark their benchmarking. They work from the premise that in a world of continuous change what they most need is to manage change, shorten the time it takes to make positive change, and bring about change that will show results with a minimum of stops and starts.

Multi-level thinkers

The thinking and mindset of the most active and successful benchmarkers also seems to function on a number of levels—often at the same time. They benchmark internally for multi-location facilities, against other firms in their industries, or against competitors in other industries.

Benchmarking for many of the most successful benchmarkers often is done regionally, on a global basis, or by best in class. But whatever way benchmarking is used they make sure there is a potential payoff. Whatever the level, they make sure their benchmarking efforts are focusing on identifying the best anywhere.

Humility pays off

Many of the most successful benchmarkers have mastered the art of convincing those who have already been through the thicket to give them some pointers. The art of winning help from those with experience is not one peculiar to benchmarkers. In fact the citation that follows tells how a young and inexperienced production chief won help from a very respected production head from another company:

"I had heard of this guy for years. He was active in several professional associations and his opinions on production and materials management were widely respected throughout the Midwest. So I got bold one day and called him up where he worked and said: Mr. xx you have the reputation for being the most professional manager in our field. Can I come and visit you some day and learn your secrets of success.

"I thought to myself that if I got a phone call like, I would have a hard time turning down a request like that. As it turned out I was right and he was incredibly helpful in showing me things he was doing in his plant. Almost immediately I began picking up a lot of good ideas. I implemented many of them very quickly.

"Later on I invited him and his people to come over and look at some of the planning and systems scheduling changes we had made or were in the process of making. Over the next two years or so I was winning recognition for some of my ideas and as a result I was able to pass a lot of good ideas to him."

What made the difference in this case had nothing to do with the requestor's knowledge and everything to do with humility.

Timing

The timing factor is often critical in presenting ideas developed in benchmarking projects. In fact, one highly successful benchmarker is so convinced of the critical nature of timing that he advises project heads that when they're developing ideas for a long range plan to be "sure to never show them to anybody. Write them down, keep them very handy, keep them locked in your top right hand drawer. Look at them every few weeks, and when business conditions warrant, start to float the ideas that are relevant. But never put too many out there at one time."

His rationale is summed up in this tale related by a corporate purchasing manager: "Early on in my career at a large Chicago-area manufacturer I had written and submitted a detailed white paper on how I saw the future for my department and the company. It was filled with ideas that I felt would be invaluable for the competitiveness of the company. Unfortunately for me, business at the time was just too good. No one wanted to rock the boat. They read my proposals, but decided not to take action.

"About a year later recession hit and the top brass began pressing all the department heads for ideas. 'What are we going to do to get back on course,' was the cry. I figured it was my time to reintroduce my white paper and recommend implementation of some specific ideas from the paper.

"They looked at my suggestions for a while, but something told me they were less than enthusiastic. Finally, the guy chairing the meeting put it on the line. 'Those are old ideas!,' he said. 'We need new, fresh, creative thinking.'

"They rejected my suggestions, of course. My mistake was floating the ideas prematurely. Later on, I had to go back and repackage the ideas with all new semantics, buzzwords, etc., and re-market them."

The moral of the tail is not so much that you should hold back ideas, but rather that you need to exercise a sense of timing. If you have come up with some ideas that can pay off over time, be careful to judge the receptiveness of those in charge. The timing may be right for the acceptance of one set of ideas, wrong for the acceptance of another set, and completely wrong for the presentation of a comprehensive plan. In fact, the' more comprehensive your plans, the more important it becomes that you exercise care in how and when new ideas are funneled into corporate thinking.

The big picture

Despite what we just said about timing, benchmarking projects don't usually happen in a vacuum. Often the most successful benchmarkers are those who are able to relate the benchmarking project to specific corporate goals and objectives. In many cases the benchmarking project is a critical cog in developing a corporate competitive strategy. For instance, how Motorola Corp.'s quality program came to be called "Six Sigma" is a good illustration of the integration of benchmarking into corporate competitive goals and objectives. (Six Sigma, by the way, is a federally registered trademark and servicemark of Motorola Inc.)

The question often is asked "Why Six Sigma and not seven? Why not five?" Actually, the Six Sigma quality initiative came about as the result of a benchmarking project. Quality status in the mid-'80s at Motorola was about on par with most other manufacturing companies in the U.S.—at about the four sigma level (around 6000 defects per million opportunities.

By the late '70s Motorola was a chastened company. Robust Far Eastern competition had forced the company to the wall and out of many of its traditional consumer electronics markets. Even its car radio market—on which the company was founded—was taken over by foreign competitors. There was Japanese competition in almost every area of its marketplace. Not only that, but even its new product markets were in danger of being overrun. As a result of all this bad news, when Motorola set out to do some benchmarking and competitive analysis in the field, there was a high degree of internal corporate interest.

Early in the benchmarking project it was learned that Japanese companies typically had quality at a five sigma level—roughly 230 parts per million defects or around 30 times fewer defects than the four sigma quality standard used by Motorola and other American companies.

In a way five-sigma was very bad news for Motorola. Even though it had pulled out of much of the consumer electronics markets and no longer had to compete against the Japanese, it was evident that the Japanese wouldn't stop there. In fact, it was evident that it was only a matter of time before the Japanese and other Far Eastern companies turned to its telecommunications and electronic markets.

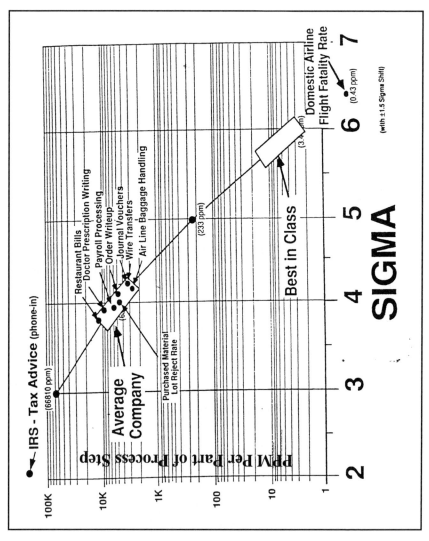

The chart on this page and the one on the next were used as illustrations in Motorola's monthly Malcolm Baldrige Award Briefings for suppliers and customers. The chart above is a generic set of illustration of the quailty of common corporate processes. The chart on the following page shows how Six Sigma plays out in terms of delivery of defect-free parts from suppliers in a typical manufacturing company.

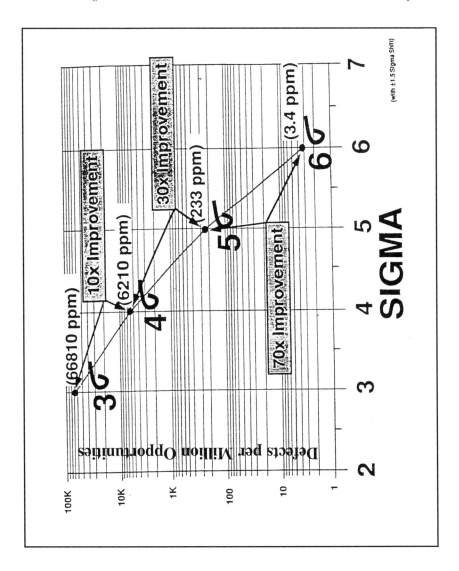

The perception was held that if any of the powerful Far Eastern electronics companies chose to compete against the remaining products in the Motorola portfolio, they could be very tough competition. Given the situation of having superior quality and low cost, they could quickly gain market share.

When benchmarkers graphed the result of a survey comparing Motorola at four sigma and potential foreign competition at five sigma, it was not a great mental leap to see that whoever got to six sigma first, would be the lowcost, high quality, high customer satisfaction supplier.

The rest, as they say, was history. Motorola chose to go Six Sigma, which required a 70 times improvement over five sigma—in essence going from roughly 230 defects per million to 3 defects per million. The point of the story is that this benchmarking analysis was incredibly helpful in winning internal Motorolans to the absolute criticality of starting from scratch toward a goal of a 70% improvement in quality.

Power counts

No matter how talented the benchmarking team, successful benchmarkers stress the absolute importance of having senior executives actively involved in the benchmarking project. As they see it such involvement enhances the quick utilization of lessons learned.

This point is driven home in the experiences of one benchmarker who earlyon in his career made a career-shaping trip to one of the pioneering companies in benchmarking. "Early in the '80s we went on a benchmarking visit to this company that practically invented benchmarking. Not only were they pioneers of benchmarking, they were also pioneers in what today we call supply chain management. What we were being exposed to was well in advance of anything we or any other companies were doing.

"They were developing strategies that had application far beyond their own field of product development. And as head of our company's benchmarking team the responsibility lay with me to say, 'What are we going to do about what we learned today? This totally changes much of the perspective we had coming into the visit!'"

"We were asking these questions early on Thursday night. Still, by Friday morning, I was able to develop an action plan based on the insights we picked up over the previous few days and present it to a division general manager. In the outline we were able to formulate some early goals, objectives, and suggested measurements, based on the insights gained from our eye-opening benchmarking visit.

"How was this possible? We had on our team a top corporate executive. His presence gave us the ability to totally change the original thrust of our benchmarking visit. In short, his presence on our team gave us the capability and flexibility to convert new knowledge to action."

The lesson here is best observed by changing things around. What, for instance, would be the outcome if only middle managers had made the trip and they did not have the understanding of its significant on a corporate level? Worse yet, what if the middle manager who headed the team had a boss who was strongly opposed to change—who had a degree of responsibility for the policies under question? How secure would the middle manager be in writing a trip report saying, "This company is much more advanced than we are and the reason is our boss rejected these ideas in the past?" One other bad alternative might be that the report writer decides not to mention anything about the truly significant stuff-saving the introduction of most of the good ideas learned for use at some unspecified later time?

Building on prior knowledge

"Don't try to boil the ocean for ideas," advises one highly successful benchmarker. More important, he and other successful benchmarkers stress the need to build on prior knowledge and acquaintenances.

Most successful benchmarkers emphasize the need to look for ideas where a principle might work for their companies, or for ideas that may be incorporated into their thinking. Many warn of the danger of looking on benchmarking as a process of writing reports that get circulated. Not nearly enough time and attention, they suggest, is spent on information—on investigating whether a principle or idea can be transferred and if so, whether its application can be expanded.

One successful benchmarker focuses on this need to look for usable ideas by entering each benchmarking session with a piece of notepaper on which two questions are written. The first says, "What are you going to do tomorrow morning? What are the one or two things you are going to do that are within your power and control (for which you don't need permission)? He reasons that if he isn't looking for those one or two priority items, then he's wasting his time.

The second question asks, What are those equally important ideas for which you do need support from others?

Without having a focus on these two questions, says the benchmarker, "we probably will return empty handed. That's because at such sessions we tend to be so busy that even though we're exposed to good ideas, we don't do anything with them. We just don't have a mechanism to force ourselves to take the next steps."

Chapter 5

PITFALLS TO AVOID

A reflection on some of the factors that most often derail benchmarking initiatives and what benchmarkers can do to avoid or minimize them.

Many—especially large—companies are incredibly naive about how quickly and effectively they can bring about change in their operations.

So in many companies, the success or failure of benchmarking is a planning and execution issue. At the top management level, for instance, there often is unprecedented interest in the fact that people haven't really looked at supply in a strategic way. They work from the basic premise that there is an unprecedented opportunity to bring benchmarking into supply management and gain an unprecedented competitive advantage to their companies. Unfortunately they often overlook the fact that there frequently are a large number of pitfalls to avoid or overcome before they can chalk up any of that competitive advantage.

Since benchmarking is at its most critical stage early on, it's important to insure that the first benchmarking programs have a high probability of success. There's nothing like early success to develop credibility and enthusiasm. Therefore, benchmarkers need to be particularly careful to minimize these two factors in taking their intial swing at benchmarking:

• **Delay.** Getting the project off the ground quickly is not merely good—it's often critical. That's because new projects are fragile. People who are a project's sponsors can quickly lose interest if it takes six months to get anything in the works.

• **Complexity.** The first project should be fairly simple or at least not overly complex. As part of this there has to be a clear economic benefit and the benchmarking project's benefits have to show up fairly quickly in the benchmarking process. Perhaps the most repeated mistake for most novice benchmarkers is biting off a project that's too big. They take on projects that are too complex and difficult for their state of preparation. Ambitious projects often need to wait for the maturation of the benchmarking team.

But while avoiding delay and undue complexity are important, they're far from being the only causes of pitfalls that await most benchmarking projects. In fact, many experienced benchmarkers can rattle off a long string of pitfalls to avoid in getting ready to launch a benchmarking project. The 10 that seem to show up most often on their lists appear in the box on page 79.

Preparation

Too frequently firms want to benchmark when they're not ready. Their conception of benchmarking is to visit some companies and talk about what the host wants to talk about. it follows, therefore, that as the result of poor preparation, members of the benchmarking team will fail to look at the things that really count.

Long before any plant visit takes place those preparing to benchmark should be asking such questions as, "Why is this company able to have this good idea in place?" Benchmarkers need to look behind the surface and keep driving questions in terms of: Why can this be done? What allows this firm to do a much better job of early sourcing, or reducing prototype development time?

Moreover, the questioning needs to follow a logical progression.

Significantly this type of thinking and questioning requires a great deal of maturation. It is not enough to know that a benchmarking partner has a good idea, it is equally important to know how it arrived at the good idea, what were the barriers they overcame, how they did it, what would they do differently next time?

In addition to wasting their own time, poorly prepared benchmarkers probably end up turning off valuable resources. They fail to recognize that the only reason a really good world-class firm would want to benchmark with them, allow them to come in and spend a number of days—two to three days, with 2-4 people on the team—is they expect something in return. And the host will only get something of value in return if the visiting firm understands the host's processes and can discuss them at a detailed level.

People make a difference

Next in seriousness and often accompanying the selection of an oversized project is staffing it with the wrong people. Too many companies want to staff projects with people they can spare rather than people who are really expert in the subject areas under study. The result of this kind of staffing is likely to be a project that is not highly successful. At worst, it may cause senior management to lose interest in process benchmarking.

Part of the issue of proper personnel selection is recognition of the fact that to do benchmarking right requires that those doing it really understand the processes involved. Without a deep understanding here, there is no way to know whether or not the company being benchmarked actually does have a better way.

Putting money where it's needed

Funding also can be a major pothole on the way to successful benchmarking. Often the heads of benchmarking initiatives allow themselves to be too tightly constrained by those holding the purse strings. For instance, it is not uncommon for top managers to say "Go ahead and do your benchmarking but stay within this greater geographical area."

While at first blush this appears to be a minor restriction, it often can kill a benchmarking initiative. A company located in Boston, for instance, can probably find out who's best in class in greater New England. But is that a sufficiently good answer? If the company is in the electronics industry it may be an acceptable restriction. If it operates in the textile industry, on the other hand, it may not be acceptable at all.

Often the cause of underfunding is simply a desire to benchmark on the cheap. Teams are allowed to do benchmarking, but they have no real travel budgets, so they are apt to discover who is good in their zip code or in a radius of 75 miles. The real benchmark of relevant best practices may be halfway around the world but these fiscally restricted benchmarkers will never know it because they are operating with severe restraints on where and with whom they can benchmark.

Why this company?

A more subtle pitfall to avoid involves perception of the target company or companies. Be sure that target companies are perceived to be successful companies by those controlling the purse strings in your company. In fact, there should be a direct correlation between perception and selection of target companies.

You want to avoid such conversations as "I know X Company is doing it, but I just read in the paper that they're laying off another 1000 workers. How do I know that what this company wants to show us isn't just another scheme to make their books look good at the expense of future growth?"

To avoid such objections, be sure to start off with a list of benchmarking candidates that are widely recognized and generally seen as successful companies. Remember, true benchmarking is not restricted to your company.

It also is a very good idea when you make a contact with a potential partner that you create a very favorable first impression, that you have established a meaningful contact, and that it would be a benefit to the target company to participate in your study. Far too many people are very clumsy in this area and they go on "fishing expeditions" that tend to overwhelm the target companies. It's very important to differentiate your project so that the intended partner thinks, "Here's an operation that really understands benchmarking, has some insights that we can profit from, and seems to have a really neat project."

You want to create a reaction that goes something like this: "We're good at what he's proposing to benchmark, but we haven't done a benchmarking project ourselves to see how good we really are. Maybe we should participate in the project because it might be a good way for us to find out how good we are today relative to others." What's in it for the other party is truly a significant issue.

Watch the numbers

It's very easy to become overly focused on the numbers. For example: One of the national professional organizations that publish benchmarking studies puts out tons of ratios. Typically it publishes ratios on such things as the cost of writing a purchase order in the petroleum industry and what is the average number of suppliers per buyer in a particular industry, etc.

The problem is that such numbers often are meaningless at best and downright dangerous in the hands of the unsuspecting or officious. For example, it is not uncommon to see companies with extremely high costs for issuing purchase orders. In one recent instance a company appeared to be spending in the range of $25,000 to write a purchase order. On face value it would not be unseemly to hear someone say, "I would never think of benchmarking with that company! They certainly aren't very efficient!"

Someone with a wider appreciation of the meaning of the figure might maintain that company is highly effective because it is able to manage supply and write very few purchase orders. The reason for the strange number is that the formula used to compute the ratio was derived by dividing the budget for the organization by the number of purchase orders issued.

Trivial issues

Failure to steer a benchmarking project to an area that is very important to senior management is a very serious mistake to make.

Clearly benchmarking should be used as a strategic process to enable a company to establish meaningful strategic goals with appropriate quantification. A benchmarking study in an area that is of little strategic importance is a waste of time, talent, and resources. Even worse, it perpetuates a misunderstanding in the minds of top management of what benchmarking should be.

Long run, trivializing the project sends an unwritten message to senior management—that it would be a negative for senior management to be personally involved. This is unfortunate, because historically the greatest beneficiaries of good benchmarking are senior executives. Often through the benchmarking process they discover that they have not been appropriately setting stretch goals and objectives for the future.

Visitation planning

Appropriate planning for a benchmarking visit is a common failing for those planning their initial benchmark project. Perhaps the most important shortcoming here is failure to develop a process for adequately analyzing what the benchmarkers will be looking at. As a result, too often teams come back from a benchmarking visit loaded down with an abundance of notes that are very difficult to weave into some meaningful conclusions.

Unless there is some way of relating the various pieces of information that are collected, much of the significance of what's collected is lost. Team members returing from a benchmarking visit too often find themselves juggling a random collection of thoughts that may or may not have meaning for their companies.

Planning for host approval

Developing plans for winning a host company's approval often can turn a benchmarking project into a swamp. Failure to plan out the goals and objectives automatically makes the benchmarking less than attractive to the potential host company.

Today, the typical prospects for a benchmarking visit are over-whelmed with project requests. Without an attractive project for the host company to participate in, it will find the door closed more often than not by the prospective host company. Mainly this is the result of failing to think through what's in it for the host company and inadequately presenting the case for becoming part of the benchmarking project.

The questionnaire

Benchmarkers often put themselves into a hole by failing to do appropriate or adequate preparation in terms of developing the questionnaire to be used in assessing internal needs and potential external ideas and answers. In addition, it's often the case that not enough of a search is carried out to identify which companies are the ones that their companies really need to be benchmarking with.

To be at peak effectiveness, a benchmarking process should be preceded well in advance by a detailed questionnaire that is focused on the subject of the benchmarking project. Unfortunately, in practice, few benchmarking projects are preceded by inquiries and/or questionnaires.

What's involved in development of a questionnaire? Basically the inquiry or questionnaire process requires locating key suppliers and customers and preparation of relevant questions that establish some basic data about customers and/or suppliers that might be used in preparing for the benchmarking project.

Typically questions are asked about such things as volumes, whether the participant has appproached the subject under study, whether it had developed standards, and whether it would be willing to share some of its findings.

DON'T START UNTIL YOU HAVE A:

• Clear understanding of what benchmarking is.

• Clear understanding of senior management's goals and expectations.

• Good information base, including measurement results, of where you stand currently on questions you plan to ask benchmarking hosts.

THE 10 DEADLY SINS

• Picking a project that lacks strategic significance, i.e. no one cares about the findings.

• Lack of in-depth preparation by those setting up the benchmarking project.

• Insufficient thought given to staffing the project, using people who can be spared, and lack of cross-functional participation.

• Lack of, or inadequate, funding of the benchmarking project.

• Haziness about the target company, its management, its accomplishments.

• Over-concentration on the numbers used in developing the benchmarking project.

• Inadequate education and training of team members.

• Not enough planning for benchmarking visits to ensure learning as much as possible.

• Insufficient planning aimed at gaining the host company's interest and participation in the project.

• Inadequate or no preparation of the inquiry or questionnaire that is used to focus on the goals of the benchmarking project.

Chapter 6

BENCHMARKING CAN BE A HARD SELL

A survey of the five main reasons companies give for not pursuing benchmarking and an analysis of their validity.

Despite great strides made in benchmarking by the world's top competitors, winning commitment for benchmarking in many corporations in America appears to be as much fun as a root canal. Where corporations have high-level management commitment and willingness to back it up financially, benchmarking progress is, indeed, being made at a rapid pace.

Best practices in a wide range of corporate processes and procurement procedures are being identified and appear to be on the way to implementation. On the other hand, the results of a recently completed mail survey and telephone poll by Purchasing Magazine of more than 500 randomly selected companies are not very encouraging.

In fact, extensive polling and interviewing revealed a lack of enthusiasm, implementation, and, in many cases, commitment to benchmarking. There also appears to be a great deal of tension on the subject itself. Many of those polled agreed to comment only when assured of anonymous attribution.

For the most part the "unreaction" to benchmarking appears to be driven by these five factors—lack of commitment at the top, lack of resources, lack of suitable partners, worries about confidentiality, and lack of understanding. Here's a point-by point look at them and how experienced benchmarkers handle them:

Lack of commitment at the top

Whether it's due to suspicion or lack of commitment, or other distractions, a fair number of respondents indicate that executive management is against benchmarking. Thus, a purchasing supervisor for a food company in California notes, "We are not permitted to benchmark because management feels competition within our industry is too great." In another case, the procurement manager for a computer storage equipment manufacturer reported that an early benchmarking effort on supplier assessment was "hopelessly muddied by management's lack of experience and commitment to benchmarking this process....They were looking for some points that could be used in a marketing program and totally derailed our benchmarking effort."

So how do you convince a senior corporate executive to look kindly on your benchmarking proposal? The unfailing approach say successful benchmarkers is to focus on money. A production manager for a Midwest farm equipment maker puts it succinctly: "They hear money every time. You have to show them this is more than some sort of showpiece program."

One successful approach for many would-be benchmarkers is via other tools such as competitive analysis or reverse engineering. If companies are in manufacturing, they probably are doing some of both and for many it's an easy link to suggesting that "we should be looking at things from the standpoint that others in our primary business are moving faster and have a better return on capital. There are some things they're doing we should consider doing that could increase our returns in this business."

Shortage of resources

In interview after interview, purchasing executives stressed the fact that their operations and their companies, overall, are running lean and under pressure to cut costs further. "Right now we don't have enough time or staff to do what we need to do," says a buyer for a large packaging company. "We'll need more staff before we can even think about benchmarking."

In most cases, say benchmarking experts, this is a cop out. Notes one dedicated benchmarker for a plastics company in New Hampshire, "All around there are opportunities to benchmark and they don't cost a king's ransom. Every day there are all kinds of opportunities to benchmark on some levels (see chart on page 88). There are trade journals, the news media, suppliers, surveys of customers and suppliers. Use of these resources don't cost much and once we start showing management the payoff, you can bet we'll get backing."

Shortage of suitable partners

For many, especially in smaller companies, the problem revolves around where to find benchmarking partners. For instance, the director of purchasing and materials management at a biotech company near Boston, notes that he still has a problem because "most companies in (his) industry lack the sophistication to be able to answer many of (his) questions."

He and many other purchasing and supply managers who were surveyed meet this problem by going outside their immediate industries. The materials manager for a small chemicals firm, for example, has solved the problem of finding suitable partners by "benchmarking on the basis of process. We ask who is best at this process and then try to set up a benchmarking study. It's a long procedure and requires much work so we have to restrict the amount of benchmarking we do." Meanwhile, the purchasing manager at a meat packing plant in Plainview, Texas, says that he is "playing catch-up" and indicates that many of his company's suppliers and competitors are "in the same situation. We're all just starting out and it's tough."

Worries about confidentiality

"Up to now, confidentiality hasn't been a problem, but I'm afraid it could be in the future," says the purchasing agent at a New Jersey electric appliance company. The purchasing director at a Florida food processing firm was more directly concerned. "We're reluctant, our management is reluctant...to share information in benchmarking. We know that we can use companies that we don't compete with, but there's still a danger that important competitive information will fall into the wrong hands."

Is this a valid concern? It is valid, but even among those who cited it as a reason for not benchmarking in Purchasing Magazine's survey, only two of those who cited confidentiality as a concern actually could cite cases where confidentiality had actually been violated.

An understanding gap

For a sizable number of respondents, benchmarking still represents an alien environment. Rather than seeking to compare their processes and procedures with the best available, they approach benchmarking in terms of averages—average inventories, average quality ratings, average number of orders processed per person, average leadtimes per class of commodity. Many other respondents candidly suggest that any benchmarking that needs to be done can be accomplished within the confines of their companies. And many fail and/or refuse to make any distinctions between processes and the functional parts of processes. In short, an alarming number of purchasing professionals have only a sketchy idea of what benchmarking is and how it works. Some are profoundly suspicious of benchmarking and its proponents, but they represent a very tiny minority.

The underlying truth that seems to emerge from the answers to this survey is that most purchasing professionals—especially those in smaller companies—are tiptoeing along the shoreline. Most buyers surveyed, even when they're not entirely sure about the mechanics of benchmarking, are for it but not necessarily ready for it. A materials manager for an Indiana capital goods manufacturer probably best sums up the mood this way: "At the moment we don't have the staff or resources to launch a major benchmarking program, but we can and are taking on one or two benchmarking projects each year. As we get better at it, we probably will do more. But right now we're just learning to walk."

Sponsors, advocates, catalysts

Finally, in seeking to win support for benchmarking or any other change process within a company, it's important to understand that there are four distinct roles. At the top is a sponsor. If you have a benchmarking idea you want to determine who you might sell it to who would be a principal sponsor. You also need advocates of this change and a catalyst or catalysts of the change. You also need to know who will be the targets of change,

Benchmarkers always have to target someone as the sponsor of benchmarking projects. Knowing who the sponsors and others that will be touched by your benchmarking project is an important part of selling the project. In addition, benchmarkers need to be aware that sponsors' needs and wants will change over time and that they will need to be able to anticipate the changes and move with the sponsor's new needs.

Despite the fact that most supply managers are not very good at selling, many who see benchmarking projects in their future will need to develop the skills of salespeople. They will need to emulate salesperson's ability to get the order.

SOURCES OF BENCHMARKING DATA

Internal information:

- Competitive product analysis.
- Reverse engineering studies.
- Company sources (sales, ex-employees).
- Other benchmarking studies.
- Internal experts and studies.

Public domain:

- Internet
- Library search (books, periodicals, journals).
- Professional networks and trade associations.
- Annual reports.
- Consultants.
- Customers.
- Suppliers.
- External experts
- Data bases.

BENCHMARKING IN INDUSTRIAL SUPPLY
(Survey of 500+ companies)

1. Does your company have a formal benchmarking program?

>YES...........................21.9%
>
>NO............................64.7
>
>SOMETIMES/INFORMAL.............14.4

2. If yes, does it use the benchmarking program to drive change?

>YES...........................75.8%
>
>NO............................15.3
>
>SOMETIMES..................... 8.8

3. How long has your company been using benchmarking?

>Under 1 year..................3.2%
>
>1-3 years....................48.4
>
>3-5 years....................25.8
>
>Over 5 years.................22.6

4. What is the main reason(s) for not doing more benchmarking?
(On a scale of 1-10)

>Lack of resources.....................7.4
>
>Lack of top management commitment......9.3
>
>Lack of suitable partners..............8.9
>
>Confidentiality concerns...............4.7
>
>Lack of understanding 5.6

SOURCE: Purchasing Magazine survey, April 1997.

Chapter 7

FINDING BENCHMARKING PARTNERS

*Success or failure in recruiting benchmarking part-
ners often owes as much to understanding than to
actual recruitment.*

In the preceding chapter we spent much time looking at the main reasons for lack of internal support for benchmarking. In this chapter we look at an even trickier problem for many would-be benchmarkers—attracting and winning benchmarking partners from other firms.

It's a major problem in many companies because it involves selling and networking skills that are often in short supply in the operational parts of the business. Selling and networking are especially important skills in winning the cooperation of best-in-class companies and organizations. As might be expected, the very best run organizations are in great demand and often need a good reason for spending valuable time with a person or organization. "What's in it for us," is a very compelling question for a company that is already best in class.

What sells benchmarking partners

Just as you need to convince your own top management of the benefits of a benchmarking project, the best potential candidates to be benchmarking partners need to be sold. They will need justification for the time expenditure in one or more of the following areas:

• The promise of information exchange that is palpable. The seller of the benchmarking project needs to convince the potential partner that there is significant information to be learned by both parties to the project.

• The potential candidate needs to be convinced that problems can be discussed frankly and in confidence. Information exchange, in other words, is not enough. It must be accompanied by analysis.

• The potential that the benchmarking project will deliver tangible results. The promise of a process improvement needs to be quantified—e.g. in terms of cost savings.

• The project will open up opportunities for knowledge exchange and learning for promising managers in the making.

Overcoming obstacles

Perhaps the biggest obstacle to overcome in securing good benchmarking partners involves overcoming ignorance about benchmarking. The fact that many people talk as if benchmarking is mainly involved with going around and looking at how other people run their operations can be a serious obstacle for someone trying to establish a benchmarking project.

Such talk and the quip, "I can't find anyone to benchmark with," are indicators of just how much work needs to be done to drive benchmarking further into the corporate consciousness. Indeed, many of the problems would-be benchmarkers have in lining up benchmarking partners appear to be the direct result of a faulty understanding of benchmarking. General ignorance and the tendency on the part of many top corporate executives to downplay the significance of benchmarking have not been helpful in further-ing the adoption of benchmarking and the search for best practices.

Judging from surveys conducted by Purchasing Magazine, not very much has been done in many companies to determine what should be analyzed in an effort to improve their own internal oper-ations. Many of the supply operations surveyed, for instance, are obviously fishing for random ideas rather than looking internally to improve the supply process. A large number see benchmarking as a tool to confirm they are on the right path rather than a tool to put them ahead in the race to best practices.

It's also apparent that a large numnber of those seeking infor-mation about benchmarking have an idea that there are great quan-tities of baseball-like statistics floating around that can be used to measure one operation against another.

What's wrong with such approaches? The main problem is that by focusing on improving numbers rather than processes they triv-ialize the benchmarking process. This kind of numbers focus does-n't tell anyone much that isn't already known. If, for instance, they know the average purchasing workload in their industry, the ratio of purchasing bodies to dollars spent, and the percent of companies in their field using supplier-rating programs, what do they really know that can help them improve their operations' processes?

Much of the ignorance problem lies with those who are cham-pioning benchmarking. Many—especially those working in supply management operations—say they often have a diffcult time con-vincing colleagues in other organizations to swap information on how they operate. Often the problem is that the would-be bench-markers are adamant that finding best practices in their field comes about only by learning how other organizational structures and lines of authority operate.

What soon becomes evident in such conversations is that many hear and use the the word "benchmarking" so often that they have developed their own mental picture of it. Unfortunately this mental picture is dead wrong and usually deals exclusively with organizational structures and the question: How do other organizations like ours operate? Somehow they miss the point that what needs to be benchmarked is how well the supply organization helps to deliver customer satisfaction. As a result, those trying to sell benchmarking are hurting their own cause by signalling that they aren't ready to deal with real issues.

Rather than worry about who reports to whom, benchmarkers in, say, a supply management organization need to consider:

• How well the supply management process controls costs.

• How quickly new products are developed and marketed.

• How well products that get to market meet customer desires.

• How well the talents of suppliers are tapped in such areas as new technology and innovation.

• How some companies have created a core competence in supply management that is a competitive advantage.

By merely dealing with organizational structures, would-be benchmarkers have a good chance of completely turning away their most promising benchmark partners. They miss the point that benchmarking is not about trying to align with a like business and copy everything it has done in an area. Rather, a successful benchmarker often needs to be looking for answers that are understood only in terms of being able to understand the partner's internal processes and current problems, planned solutions, etc..

Questions for the in-house operation

They also have to be aware that for the most part, readily transferrable good-ideas are not that common. In fact, a would-be benchmarker would be well advised to turn to his or her own internal operation with questions like these:

• **The buy.** Is what we are buying today truly what's needed? Or is it only the result of compromises made in the past for reasons that are no longer valid? What needs to change?

• **Suppliers.** Are our prime suppliers really world class? How do their processess match up with ours? Are their technological/production capabilities sufficient for our future needs?

• **The supply chain.** Do the pieces of the supply chain actually fit together? Are the suppliers' suppliers good enough for the level of service expected from them? How good are the links between design, manufacturing, procurement, marketing? Are our own suppliers effectively managing their own Tier One suppliers—and down the supply chain?

• **Changing conditions.** Is what we make, is how we do business, the best possible for current business conditions? Where should we be looking for new ideas? What new technology needs to be explored? How should our relationships with suppliers cha

• **Monitoring.** How good and timely are our supplier performance metrics? Do they actually measure what needs to be measured? Are they effective?

• Are we a world class customer that earns and receives preferential support from our suppliers?

Once the benchmarker has dealt with these kinds of questions at home, he/she is in a better position to truly understand and use all the good information that is available from the benchmarking partner. Most important, it plays a fundamental part in attracting smart people from smart companies into setting up a benchmarking project.

If after taking measures to improve your understanding of

benchmarking, you still can't find a benchmark partner, does that mean you can't benchmark? The answer is an emphatic, "no." The simple fact is that if you can look at things in terms of basic principles, then you can learn useful things and develop useful insights by studying the processes of your company and other companies.

On winning trust

Getting and keeping good benchmarking partners also involves a number of confidentiality issues. To really be good at building benchmarking partnerships requires that you build up some trust. For the long term there has to be a build-up of rapport where people feel comfortable and free to say things off the record.

One significant way to establish this trust is through active acceptance of the benchmarker's code of conduct (see page 210). The code, adopted by the Strategic Partnering Institute, the International Benchmarking clearinghouse, and the Benchmarking Exchange spells out acceptable standards of confidentiality, legality, information exchange, information use, preparation, first-party contact conventions, and third-party contact conventions. It goes a long way in breaking down fears that confidentiality is compromised in benchmarking.

Is it possible to benchmark without actually having formal benchmark partners? This question often comes up in discussions about how hard it is to develop benchmarking partnerships.

The problem with the question is that it represents a variation on the theme that is less benchmarking and more scanning the environment for what's going on. Benchmarking really implies that one company is going to examine a problem or problems with another company it respects as a successful company. Analysis alone isn't necessarily benchmarking. It's a collection of facts and an effort to make some conclusions, but it lacks the personal interaction that differentiates benchmarking from most of the analytical tools in use today.

A partner implies a flow of trust that allows for people to reach beyond the norm. It's an expected part of the interaction for interchanges like, "You're good at this...how did you get there? What were the pitfalls enroute?...If you were to recreate this capability, what would you do differently the second time?...The third time?... Say, who is the person who sold this? Does he still work for your company?"

Who's doing it?

One hurdle in recruiting benchmarking partners is the reluctance of people and organizations to be pioneers—to be first in the field. As Michael E. Porter notes in his book "The Competitive Advantage of Nations," change is an unnatural act, particularly in successful companies; powerful forces are at work to avoid it at all costs." When a subject like benchmarking arises, people get edgy and tend to look around and note that no one in their immediate region is doing it (benchmarking)—so naturally they don't want to be the first ones in the field!

Porter, of course, is only echoing what Niccolo Machiavelli so aptly penned more than 500 years ago, "There is nothing more difficult to attempt, more perilous to conduct, or more uncertain in its success, than to take the lead in the introduction of a new order of things...because the innovator has for enemies all those who have done well under old conditions, and only lukewarm defenders in those who might do well under the new."

In failing to champion an idea like benchmarking these timid souls fail to take into account that there is great value in being the first one in an industry or a geographic location to apply benchmarking. There are some significant benefits that followers don't have. The most important, to quote an old agricultural aphorism, is they get the "pick of the litter" in lining up best in class partners.

Benchmarking and the legend of Sam Walton

Perhaps the most overlooked factor in finding benchmarking partners is the recognition that it can be profitable to benchmark with non-manufacturing firms. In fact, it should be noted that a growing number of non-manufacturing companies are doing the heavy lifting in developing benchmarking insights and applying benchmarking to problem solving. Non-manufacturing companies often use processes that are similar to their manufacturing cousins. Perhaps more important, many non-manufacturing operations often use and look at their processes in ways that differ radically from straight manufacturing industries—often in ways that offer new creative insights.

For some perspective on what you might expect in ideas from non-manufacturing operations, witness the benchmarking history of the all-time champion benchmarker—Wal-Mart. Perhaps the most successful of all non-manufacturing benchmarkers, the Wal-Mart chain of self-service discount super stores has a history of benchmarking that has lessons for everyone.

Back around 1960 when Wal-Mart's founder Sam Walton had one "five and dime" store, a bank debt, and everyone else trying to run him out of business, he read in a trade journal about two experimental stores in Minnesota that were doing self-service retail discounting.

As the head of a company too small to allow for delegating, Walton decided to take a look at the operation on his own. So he bought an overnight bus ticket from Bentonville, Ark., to Minnesota. He spent the entire day with a yellow legal pad taking copious notes and returned to Bentonville. Not long after that he opened a third such discount store—and then a fourth and a fifth. Today there are more than 3000 Wal-Mart stores with sales that exceed $125 billion and all of Walton's competition has been left in his wake.

It's an exceptional example of a small company using the concept of learning from others and building it into an absolute mantra for how it runs. Today Wal-Mart's managers still travel around the country benchmarking wherever they think they can pick up ideas that can be used in their company. The only difference from the early days is that they travel in company planes so they can cover more territory. Even today they are methodically soaking up better ways to do things via benchmarking.

Over the years Wal-Mart managers have followed Sam Walton's example of setting goals and developing priorities. Early on Wal-Mart took cross-docking to new levels of sophistication because it was seen as a significant step in reaching Walton's goal of always being the low price provider. Often there weren't many alternatives in setting goals. The main ones involved managing supply, because these enabled Wal-Mart to compete with companies that were much larger.

Wal-Mart managers examined cost elements in managing supply. A big one for the company was logistics, which affected the company's whole expansion strategy. As a result of recognizing logistics' importance early, the company never outran its own logistics system. It built warehouses as needed to meet its expansion strategy. As warehouses were added, new stores could follow.

Gradually as this expansion kicked in, the company was able to develop greater leverage with suppliers. As a growing player in the retail market, Wal-Mart's business became more important to its suppliers. Over the years Wal-Mart also did creative things with suppliers in such areas as packaging and promotions. Over time it had suppliers managing their own shelf space—thus reducing Wal-

Mart's overhead structure. Then Walton made large strategic investments in information systems that currently are a core competence and long-term competitive advantage.

By constant benchmarking Wal-Mart came to realize how little its competitive strategy depended on transactions and how much it depended on areas that its competitors were still wrestling with. As a result, purchasing people found that their jobs were changed. Where once they were primarily concerned with processing transactions, today they are primarily concerned with adding value from a supplier management aspect.

Sam Walton started off with a mindset that no one knows all there is to know, that there's value in looking to the outside world and picking up ideas that might work in his operation. He was especially concerned with getting away from the "not invented here" syndrome where companies say "we're different, how can we ever learn anything from them?"

Chapter 8

MEASURING RESULTS

How many ways a company has for measuring performance is far less important than developing measures that drive real process change.

One of the most important elements in successful benchmarking is effective measurement systems. Indeed, benchmarking flows from measurements, from conclusions drawn from measurements, from new goals developed from conclusions. How well this all fits together depends on how well the measurements link to the strategic direction of the company. Unfortunately measurement tends to be a very weak area for most companies—especially in their supply management processes.

Nevertheless, the need to establish appropriate measures of performance is particularly apparent in firms where the importance of sourcing has increased significantly in recent years. In companies with higher variable costs and relatively low direct labor costs, for instance, the need to control and manage supply costs has become more urgent as external suppliers account for growing percentages of a finished product's value. The need for improved, relevant sourcing and supply management measurements are notably on the rise:

• In firms that purchase many critical items from a standpoint of quality and technology. As they increase the criticality of components, systems, and materials, quality problems can begin to increase marketplace dangers.

• In companies where using inappropriate technology has a potential to reduce the product's value in the eyes of the customer.

• In businesses where there is increasing pressure to bring new products to the market faster.

• In businesses needing to reduce the time and cost of new product development programs.

For a growing number of companies the changing relationship between buying and selling companies is driving supply managers to come up with better measurement systems. In many cases the degree of interdependence is growing between buying companies and the firms in their value/supply chains. Increasing dependence on suppliers for technology is being matched by an increasing dependence on the part of suppliers to get customers to try out new technology. Such interdependencies require better measurement systems.

Measures needed to drive change

Perhaps the most important driver behind the push for better measurements in the sourcing-supply function is the lack of measures that drive continuous improvement and change people's behavior. Unfortunately many of the measurements now in place don't measure the things that count in competition. In many companies performance of the sourcing/supply function is still mainly a matter of conformance to one or more purchase price variance systems. The problem is that just meeting a standard cost in a standard environment in order to achieve a budgeted cost reduction level doesn't mean much. Such measurements are tied to holding the status quo, not achieving breakthrough levels.

Another major failing with many measurement systems is they focus subjectively and infrequently on such things as supplier delivery and quality performance. In most cases these ineffective approaches fail to measure and identify what truly needs to be done to improve performance.

In a similar vein, many measurement systems in place today emphasize efficiency rather than effective performance. Instead of aiming at sourcing/supply policy objectives, for instance, they concentrate on transaction processing measures. Best in class companies are heavy users in electronic commerce as a means of cutting cycle time and transportation costs

The real question that needs to be asked about performance measurement systems is: Do they align with the competitive realities of what people in supply management need to do in order to compete today? In most cases the answer is "no"—the measurements supply managers are using do not align with their responsibilities or the expectations of their firms' top executives.

Another weakness of most measurements in play today is they don't prod people into looking at integration among different functional activities and organizations. In many companies the reality is that there are no measures that provide for seamless kinds of activities among procurement, product/process engineering, manufacturing, scheduling, etc. As a result the measures contribute nothing toward bringing about departmental integration.

Driving behavior

Many supply managers are working to develop measures that drive behavior toward achieving what is required in today's business environment. For example, instead of only using purchase price variance, in many product areas there may be a need to use target prices for a commodity, component, subassembly, or system as a measurement. The desired behavior is to drive the best in class design to meet the target price—so that the firm can compete when it introduces a new product. This is especially important in short product life-cycle situations. In such cases firms often need to come to market with prices that are competitive and, where possible, have time to go back and take out an additional percentage of cost. Chrysler became so good at this that it was acquired by Daimler-Benz as a means of spreading the process into the new parent.

In many companies reforms will need to begin in the production process to link total cost improvement measures just as if they were unit price reduction measures. Measures of manufacturing cost reduction will need to cover far more than general purchase price. They will need to include other costs related to doing business that are influenced by suppliers—including such items as labor costs and and recycling costs.

On the supplier side, measures of supplier development are needed that indicate how well individual suppliers are performing. Measures need to capture whether suppliers are improving both their capabilities and performance. Performance measurements can and should relate to quality and delivery performance, but they also need to relate to improvement in terms of supplier capabilities and total lowest cost.

Also needed are measures that gauge the contribution suppliers are making to cost, quality, and technology improvement. If companies are asking supplier partners to make value engineering-value analysis contributions to a product, then there needs to be ways to measure the groups that have responsibility for driving that VA/VE performance and what suppliers are contributing. Over the product life cycle firms need to ask suppliers to come in with suggestions relating to such things as design and manufacturing costs and cost of doing business.

Chrysler's SCORE program

Chrysler Corp. boasts an an excellent example of this application of measurements to benchmarking principles in its SCORE program. Suppliers working in the company's SCORE program know that if they want to retain or grow their business with Chrysler, they must find innovative ways to reduce cost. They also know that they will get to split the savings with Chrysler.

Under SCORE (Supplier Cost Reduction) Chrysler taps into the expertise of its suppliers to cut costs. Suppliers are invited to submit ideas based on their experiences with other OEMs. Proposals are evaluated to assure that there is no degradation of quality and that the supplier and Chrysler are on the same page so far as the computation of the actual cost savings

Evaluations and feedback on the proposals are handled on an expedited basis. As a result, even though proposals are routed internally to all the players on Chrysler's evaluation team, response back to the supplier is relatively speedy.

Each year Chrysler receives a wide variety of proposals—ranging from the employment of new lower cost manufacturing technology to the use of different lower-cost materials.

While SCORE is not mandated by Chrysler, it has become part of the business relationship between the auto company and its suppliers. In fact, it is part of Chrysler's supplier rating system. Suppliers' SCORE performance is evaluated three ways:

• **Annualized savings.** What is the percentage of approved savings compared to the amount of business Chrysler gives to the supplier.

• **Batting average.** How many of the supplier's proposals are implemented compared to the number the supplier presented?

• **Other suppliers.** How many proposals has the supplier submitted compared to the rest of the supply base?

What measurements are needed?

The trouble with talking about the long list of things measurements need to address in general and the measurement criteria needed to get benchmarking off the ground is that they aren't necessarily the same. On the one hand we're talking about ideal measurements—for corporate competitors in general. But as we note elsewhere in this book, most initial and early benchmarking projects have relatively modest objectives and scope.

Typically benchmarking project teams run into trouble determining just exactly what measurements are needed for the project. Representatives from the various integrated functions tend to want to layer on more and more measurements. As each function makes its recommendations the search for appropriate measures turns into an exercise in self congratulation—where departments promote adoption of measures where they look good and try to ignore ones where they don't.

In most benchmarking projects what needs to be concentrated on are the key initiatives that the corporate fathers say are most important. Measurements need to flow out of key beliefs, goals, and initiatives. The important thing is to boil all the conflicting interests of the various functions down into the important few measures that reflect the cororate strategy. Not until this is done is it possible to have a common language that the team can use in determining the relative success and failure of the project.

It's considerable work to boil the measures down to the essential ones, but the exercise is invaluable in highlighting the linkage back to the strategic plan. A good argument for using this approach is that as the strategic plan changes it's possible to go back and change some of the measures without derailing the whole process.

Sometimes, despite the need to show early results, it's necessary to develop a comprehensive set of measures. This is especially important where a benchmarking project is executed across multi units of the company. At Motorola, for instance, boiling down the measurements that would be used to a manageable few took more than a year. The corporate supply management council in 1990 eventually came up with the key measures that were universal across the entire corporation for supply management. The measures traveled all the way to the corporate chief operating officer from each division. In the end there were only six measures, but they tied back to Motorola's corporate-wide goals.

Corporate fathers had laid down the key initiatives that they felt were at the bottom of what they wanted to work on. Each of the key measures flowed out of key beliefs, key goals, key initiatives of the company. Adopting the six key measures won the supply managers high credibility with management. And winning management approval for the standard measurements made it possible to apply Six Sigma principles across the company and its suppliers.

Measurement essentials

Finally, what about the general process of developing more effective measurement systems? What do companies really need to consider when they put the measurements they live by under the microscope? Here's one seven-step approach being used by a number of companies:

• **Decide what's needed.** Firms first need to determine what's needed to compete and how supply management will play a role in that competition. Do they see themselves in the role of the low-cost producer? Or, perhaps, they see their distinctive competency in terms of time, technology, or value. Whatever competitive role a firm chooses to play, it will need a supply base and supply system that is capable of maximixing the choice by giving different weights to various effectiveness (vs. efficiency) measures.

• **Determine behavior.** It will be necessary to establish the kinds of behaviors needed, by whom (sourcing and supply, manufacturing, engineering), and how these behaviors will reinforce the competitive plan. If team behaviors need to be reinforced, measures will need to be drawn up that focus on what the team needs to achieve in terms of technology and time. If the need is to drive down product costs over a long product life cycle, then measurements will need to emphasize on-going cost reduction.

If the way to achieve on-going cost reductions is through negotiations, then the measurements will put a big burden on supply management. If value engineering is envisioned as the primary way to achieve on-going cost reductions, then measurements will need to span the cross-functional scene. Those developing measurements will need to establish what procedures are necessary and then begin to assign measures to the appropriate level—to the individual or to the group. As part of this measurement development, it may also be necessary to establish a supplier cost improvement suggestion measure and supplier development process measures.

• **Draw up a measurements profile.** In the course of determining behaviors, it often will be necessary to establish a business profile. Are we a high volume producer? A low-volume one? Is the product mix high or low? Is the product cycle long or short? On what basis do we compete? Each profile will require a specific behavior that needs to be emphasized and measures to help the firm compete.

Each company needs to profile the business and then develop the specific measures unique to it that are focused to support competitiveness. Many of the measurements will relate to quality, technology, cost, total cost, total value, delivery, and flexibility. But the individual measurements will differ, depending on their relative significance to each company and at what level they're to be applied (individual or team).

• **Review the current system.** Once it has been decided what behaviors need to be emphasized in achieving a company's competitive goals, it's time to look at the current performance evaluation and rewards system in relation to the company's needs. It's necessary to see if the evaluation and rewards system is alligned correctly in terms of using the right measurements to emphasize either individual or team performance.

For example, if it's necessary to emphasize team performance in the new product development phase and every measure for engineering, manufacturing, and procurement is an individual measure, the right kind of behavior will not be emphasized. If, for instance, people see they're not being rewarded for spending 25% of their time on a team, and getting penalized for not doing other parts of their job that are individually measured, they'll very likely conclude that teamwork doesn't pay. It's very necessary to establish the component of the measurement that will be done individually, but supervised, and that which will be done on a team basis and by which people.

• **Alignment.** Once the review is completed, it's necessary to quickly establish the appropriate measures as indicators of performance and realign the rewards system so that it benefits in terms of salary, recognition, and short-term bonuses will reflect what has happened at both the individual and team level.

• **Analyze the process.** Based on the effectiveness measures being used and behaviors required, it's necessary to examine the strategies and processes needed to achieve performance and fix problems. The process can be enhanced by understanding and applying the "most advanced strategies and practices" used world-

MEASUREMENTS LINKED TO STRATEGIC PLAN AND KEY BELIEFS

Key beliefs—how we will always act:

- Constant respect for people.

- Uncompromising integrity.

Key goals—what we must accomplish:

- Increased global market share.

- Best in class people, marketing, technology, product, manufacturing, service.

- Superior financial results.

Key Initiatives—how we will do it:

- Six Sigma quality.

- Total cycle time reduction.

- Product and manufacturing leadership.

- Profit improvement.

- Participative management within, and cooperation between organizations.

New supply management measures:

1. Supplier quality—line fallout ppm.

2. Material cost savings—actual to actual

3. Supplier profile—(Are we walking the talk?)

4. Supplier on-time delivery %

5. Total manufacturing inventory turns.

6. Supplier critiques of Motorola.

At Motorola, corporate executives laid down the key initiatives they felt were needed as part of the company's thrust to achieve Total Customer Satisfaction. Adoption of key measurements were linked directly to how well Motorola was meeting key beliefs, goals, and initiatives.

wide. Performance measures are indicators of process effectiveness, thus processes and measures both need to be modified.

• Review. It's necessary to regularly review the process to see if what's being called for in the competitive environment is changing. Unless firms are willing to step up to this issue, they may find they're using outdated measures and processes that result in outdated approaches that limit their ability to compete.

PURPOSE OF PERFORMANCE MEASUREMENT

Motivate behavior that leads to continuing improvement in:

- Quality/customrer satisfaction.

- Productivity.

- Cost.

- Flexibility.

Widely communicate major objectives.

THE LOGIC OF GOOD MEASUREMENTS

- Success requires change.

- Change requires new behaviors.

- New behaviors require new measurement and reward system.

- Trashing obsolete emeasures is an early step toward success.

- Installing appropriate new measures accelerates progress toward success.

Section 1

THE BENCHMARKING SCENE

How benchmarking sometimes gets a bad name...Benchmark your insourcing...Purchasing as a core competence...Getting out of the batter's box...A young person's take on how to use and not use "best practices"...Benchmarking could save sourcing from being outsourced...How benchmarking mindset pays off...Benchmarking grows up... Benchmarking! Who should do it?

How benchmarking sometimes gets a bad name

Benchmarking is probably the most misunderstood, poorly used idea to come down the road in recent years. It's name is partly at fault; benchmarking sounds like something done to inanimate objects, for example, a computer systems comparison. Also problematic are published reports—purporting to be benchmarking—that show primarily ratios of purchasing's clerical efficiency'

True benchmarking focuses on results in such areas as supplier quality, productivity improvement (i.e. reduced pricing), and supplier responsiveness.

I prefer the term "continuous comparison" to reflect ongoing, focused reviews evaluating your status against comparable processes, products, and functions. Continuous comparison should be very personal as we quantify, assess, and compare our management prowess against our peers in competing firms. Obviously care must be exercised to insure we are comparing apples to apples. No executives—not even CEOs—should be exempt.

Ten years ago the late Pete Landry, formerly of Xerox, made a lasting impression on me with these views of benchmarking:

- **Rigor.** Ensure that improvement targets are set high enough.

- **Overcoming disbelief.** Convince yourself you can do better.

- **Accountability.** Establish an ongoing process for measuring performance and insuring improvement.

- **Culture change.** Look outward instead of inward. I have developed an improvement model that should be employed sequentially in a successful TQM process.

- **Step One:** Hear the primary, prioritized needs of key customers. This is an opportunity to win business from the competition.

- **Step Two:** Compare how well your firm meets key customer needs. Include a comparison with the competition.

- **Step Three:** Learn from others through this process. For example, is Company A's performance better? Why? What can we learn? How can we apply what we have learned?

- **Step Four: Improve:** Results only come if we take actions to improve performance in areas that are important to customers.

- **Step Five: Return to Step One.** This is a closed-loop process.

Many purchasing functions today are under the scrutiny of business-process re-engineering projects. This is particularly true in departments that are still oriented toward transaction processing and procedure manuals. Their customers and management see their work as clerical non-value added activity. I hope that I have sounded a note of caution to those interested in the average number of requisitions processed by buyers in their SIC code.

VALUE OF BENCHMARKING

RIGOR

MAKE SURE THAT THE TARGETS
ARE SET HIGH ENOUGH.

OVERCOMING DISBELIEF

CONVINCING OURSELVES THAT
WE CAN DO BETTER.

ACCOUNTABILITY

AN ONGOING PROCESS FOR
MEASURING PERFORMANCE
AND ENSURING IMPROVEMENT.

CULTURAL CHANGE

AN OUTWARD LOOKING
COMPANY RATHER THAN ONE
WHICH IS INTERNALLY FOCUSED.

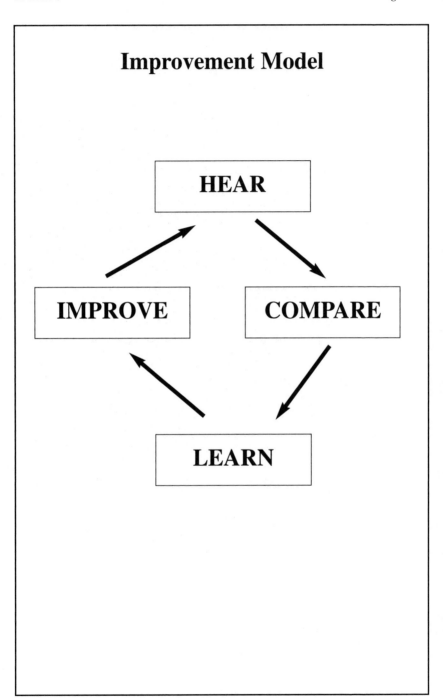

Improvement Model

HEAR

IMPROVE   **COMPARE**

LEARN

Benchmark your insourcing

Reengineering—the national fad of the decade—has good news, bad news implications. Good news is that unemployment in the consulting profession has been significantly diminished. Bad news is that the purchasing process is a favorite target and many excellent purchasing people lose their jobs on the altar of efficiency due to outsourcing, credit card procurement, integrated suppliers, JIT II, etc.

Anyone who is not a proactive champion of improvement and change deserves to be outsourced. However, I would like to suggest for your consideration a continuous comparison-benchmarking project on insourcing. How much money is spent by your company outside the purchasing-supply management function, and how effectively and intelligently is it spent?

I recall a situation where information services (IS) in a large company spent millions on hardware, software, telephone services, etc. Users of their services faced increased budget charges year after year. IS managers haughtily dismissed overtures for purchasing to join a team seeking possible ways to reduce internal costs as seen by users.

A new IS director finally agreed to a test project. One Friday afternoon, the purchasing director received a call advising him that he could look for an RFQ and contribute his ideas, as long as the RFQ was mailed within two hours. He quickly scanned the cover letter and the two-pound RFQ earmarked for three suppliers.

The purchasing director suggested insertion of a simple paragraph in the cover letter to the effect that telecommunications services were currently purchased among three suppliers and that the company intended to reduce its supplier base. As a result, the successful bidder would receive an 80% share—possibly 100% of the business. The phone bill fell sharply thereafter.

What are the insourcing opportunities in your organization? Learn from those who already have won some internal skirmishes. But don't start a project until management demonstrates some interest. You'll no doubt have valid answers, but credibility is greater when the answers arise after management tells you to "find out how we compare."

Purchasing as a core competence

Most progressive companies are taking a fresh look at processes related to customer and supplier relationships, and this creates a huge opportunity. One measure is executive search activity, and target compensation for a new hire. Another is benchmarking or continuous comparison activities. Consulting and project backlogs also are a growing sign of significant change.

Behind these outcroppings of optimism lie some fundamental changes in the thinking associated with supply and procurement. To wit:

• Many companies realize that for many years the purchasing function has not been seen as a critical success factor. Recommendations for improvement (change) suggested by the head purchaser were generally not implemented.

• Purchasing was—and often still is—a sub-set of another function, typically manufacturing. Job security improves for the subordinates who focus on helping the boss meet his goals. Purchasing should be general manager-external manufacturing, not a sub-activity of internal manufacturing.

• Modern masnufacturing practices have frequently led to highly automated factories where purchased materials represent the major expense, 70% or more of a product's total cost. In such cases, it would make more sense to have manufacturing report to a supply management executive. In a growing number of companies, the senior supply executive is a peer of the classical functions: manufacturing, sales, finance.

• Many companies recognize the tremendous value of early supply involvement in new product design. Speed to market is a widely recognized critical success factor. A supply management pro who can garner early access to critical supplier expertise is a rare commodity in high demand today.

• Everyone in recent years has fancied himself or herself as a purchasing pro. Growing evidence today illustrates the financial folly of letting amateurs spend large sums of shareholders' money. The first step of insourcing should be to know who controls what portions of total dollars spent.

Getting out of the batter's box

Many readers of this book are probably familiar with the benchmarking studies conducted by the Center for Advanced Studies in Tempe, Ariz. A recent report on the petroleum industry cites some mathematical averages showing that—surprise—buyers are doing more work with fewer resources, head counts, budgets, etc.!

These studies appear to view purchasing strictly as a function, and they compute averages on efficiency (?) in a supply group. I see no reference in these studies to the "acquisition process," where purchasing people should play a key role in a cross-functional endeavor.

For those readers who think this is true benchmarking, they are likely to strike out and be sent back to the bench, banished forever in the minor leagues, or thrown out of the game entirely.

Many readers are familiar with *Industry Week*'s annual competition for the 10 best plants award. As part of the competition, the magazine publishes a statistical profile of information representing accomplishments in finalist companies. It covers all aspects of plant operations and the information on supplier partnership (a process) is a good start on a benchmarking process for many readers. Some excerpts I can share:

• In finalist companies, 20 suppliers equal 80% of spending on purchased material.

• One hundred percent of finalists emphasize early supplier involvement.

• Eighty percent of the finalists ask critical suppliers to rate their performance as customers.

• Sixty-four percent of finalists embrace design for procurement, a hot button of mine.

What are the answers in your company? In today's world all of us must be able to show we add value to processes that are important.

A young person's take on how to use and how not to use 'best practices'

One of the advantages of being a grandparent is you can have long conversations about a lot of things without getting bogged down in discipline and such.

I had such a conversation recently with my granson, Phillip. He started first grade recently and I decided to hold a conversation about my first love—benchmarking. I was surprised at how easily he grasped the idea that benchmarking is a continuous process of seeking out best practices in successful organizations in their products, services, and work processes.

To test his understanding I asked him why he thought a company that was already successful and busy would want to set aside time and resources to study other organizations. His answer was short and to the point: "So they can do better even faster."

Then I asked him what he has learned in his young life, to do when he discovers that he is behind a competitor in an important area. He thought a bit and came up with four options.

First, was the option to work harder and longer. This didn't seem practical to him, because it didn't seem to change anything.

A second option was to emulate the best practices of your most advanced competitor. This, he felt, was better than the first, but still left you "behind—only not so far behind...But if you haven't looked at him (the competitor) lately, you may be way behind because he's added something since you last looked at him," said Phillip

His third option showed me just how perceptive even young children can be. He couched this option in terms of "leapfrogging" beyond the best practices of the most advanced competitor. His explanation of how this can be done was in terms of his first passion—soccer. As he explains it, he studies other players' habits and skills and frequently can successfully anticipate where the ball will go. "Most of my 11 goals came from being in the right place," he said.

I told Phillip this was a great example and was similar to how Chrysler and its platform team process has leapfrogged everyone to become the most profitable car maker in the world.

But Phillip wasn't finished. He listed an option that can put you so far ahead that your competitors may never catch up—"change the rules of the game." He was right, of course. That's exactly what Sam Walton did at Wal-Mart. He built a core competence in low cost logistics and supply management, resulting in low prices to

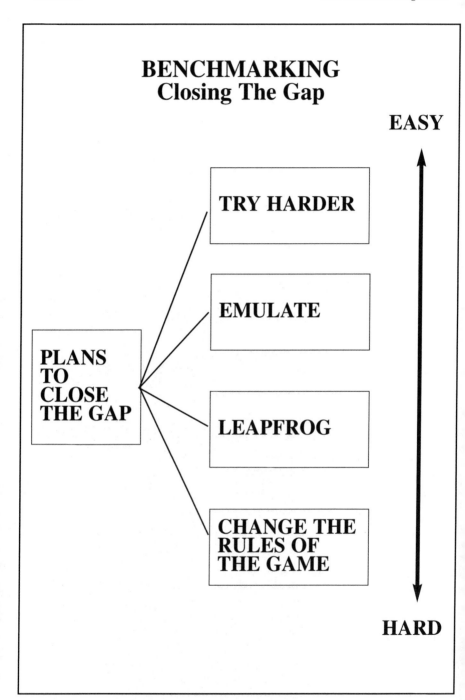

the customer and above-average profits to the company.

One thing we didn't get around to in our conversation: It isn't enough to set appropriate goals and pursue them. There must be an objective means of measuring progress to determine whether goals are being achieved. Without measurement, goals are merely a statement of good intentions that everyone can agree to, and for which no one can be held accountable.

Benchmarking could save sourcing from being outsourced

Recently I attended a meeting and listened to an interesting presentation on a newly formed firm focusing on outsourcing. The founder of the new firm has been heavily involved in outsourcing many activities at a large diversified firm. Pride was very apparent in the retelling of how many national contracts were leveraged and a great deal of money was claimed to have been saved.

During a question and answer session, meeting attendees learned that today the story wasn't so rosy at that prior employer. All the purchasing staff had been outsourced (their jobs were eliminated and the people became suddenly unemployed). The national contracts then quickly deteriorated because there were no resources left at the buying customer to manage the supply and supplier relationship.

The presenter continued to emphasize how her new firm focused totally on helping large companies to outsource major, nonproductive purchases. Phase two in the helping stage was to enable clients to eliminate their purchasing departments! I found that fascinating as the presenter was a recent victim of what she was planning to do to others.

Readers, this is not an isolated situation. A very large consulting firm has a current search underway for a principal to build a consulting practice "through outsourcing the sourcing/procurement process for major multinationals."

This may be a good time to conduct a review of how you and the processes you lead and manage add value to your company. This is a potential benchmarking project that could be very valuable in the future to you and your company.

I continue to believe and advocate that supply management needs to be developed into a core competence in many companies. This is an obvious part of my mindset, and I am confident of my position, even though a growing number of businesses are committed to profiting from the elimination of procurement staffs.

How benchmarking mindset pays off

I recently came across an outstanding example of how to harness and use the potential power of the benchmarking process. It's contained in a CEO's letter to shareholders in his company's annual report.

The corporation, for a number of years, has relentlessly pursued a goal that each major business group must become number one or two in its respective markets and must show consistent annual improvement. Clearly these are aggressive, stretch goals.

The value system the CEO has chosen is what we call benchmarking. To quote: "Our behavior is driven by a fundamental core belief that the desire and ability of an organization to continuously learn from any source, anywhere—and to rapidly convert this learning into action—is the ultimate competitive advantage."

The author then went on to explain how his company had successfully reduced the many barriers impeding effective knowledge re-use. Among the major things it did was to—

• Roam the world, benchmarking others to learn their best practices.

• Establish rewards—career and financial—for those people willing to participate in the change process.

• Revise management appraisal and compensation systems to support the new value systems and long-term objectives.

This best practice example is from General Electric, a hugely successful company, by any measure.

Benchmarking grows up

Benchmarking continues to survive and prosper as a change-management tool in many companies due to more sophisticated and strategic use of the process. In fact, it is possible to track the progress of these sophisticated or advanced benchmarkers through a three-stage maturation process:

• **Stage 1.** Benchmarking generally started with primary quantitative content (80-90%) versus just 10-20% qualitative content. In essence, the focus was on numbers, ratios, costs, etc. Relatively small attention was paid to how the numbers were derived, improved, or formed trends over time. And benchmarking partners tended to be from the usual list of high profile firms (Baldrige Award winners, cover stories in *Purchasing Magazine, Business Week, Fortune*, etc.). Data orientation tended to be comparative, e.g. Wal-Mart turns its inventory X% faster than Kmart without explanation of how and why this was achieved.

• **Stage 2.** Benchmarking began to change in committed, sophisticated companies. Content reversed to an 80-90% focus on process versus 10-20% quantitative. They had a growing interest in best practices, but all too frequently, they had an orientation to local or nearby benchmarking partners. Data was generally oriented to descriptive terms.

• **Stage 3.** This is where most advanced benchmarkers are today. Content or focus is 80% on process, 10-20% on strategy, and quantitative is 0-10%. They are frequently successful in forming a network of benchmarking partners that truly represent best practices in the topic area. Their search for benchmarking partners is worldwide. They have something of value to offer a potential benchmarking partner: admittance to their network on a specific topic area and access to the project final report—if they participate. These final reports contain considerable prescriptive information that can be of strategic value to all participants.

Newcomers to the benchmarking process obviously wish to gain access to key people in best practice organizations at Stage 3. But they may have little of value to offer their target partners. If the target individuals perceive that you are at Stage 1, you will very likely be unable to gain access to them and their companies' knowledge, strategies, advice, and counsel.

Benchmarking! Who should do it?

You may be thinking: "Okay, I'm convinced. Benchmarking is a good thing to do...but I'm really busy. Just tell me how I should approach this specific need for credible information on how good we really are in sourcing and managing our supplier relationships. In essence we want to benchmark the effectiveness of our organization."

One alternative is to hire a consultant to conduct a study and report back to you on its findings. I recently received a phone call advising me of a desired study on purchasing effectiveness in a large corporation. The potential client has a long history of being widely regarded as a high cost provider.

When I received a fax covering the desired scope of work it turned out to be a call for an industry survey on prices paid for common use items routinely purchased in its specific industry and how its actual prices paid compared to others.

Was this a credible way to measure the effectiveness of that purchasing organization? Probably not! That's because the common items to be surveyed represented less than 1% of the firm's cost to produce its product. Purchasing, in the industry, historically plays a minor role in selecting sources, developing specifications, and controlling supply to minimize inventories. Its role is concentrated in the transaction area.

I proposed a different approach, but one more likely to result in a measure of effectiveness. I offered to assist the firm in identifying specific, relevant best practices from leading organizations outside its industry. If it was the first to implement these processes in its industry, then it should quickly see the cost gaps begin to narrow.

The company, however, is proceeding on a third-party cost study and management has declined to become personally involved. This is a mistake. By venturing out personally to understand best practice companies, you can quickly gauge your strengths and weaknesses. You may see that your company and your industry are years behind other industries. But these gaps won't close until department heads and other key executives learn that they are part of the problem. Hiring a consultant or sending a subordinate with a mortgage and kids in college is not likely to result in an accurate assessment of how you compare to a best practice company. Not knowing where you are is a terrible price to pay.

Section 2

WHAT BENCHMARKING IS ABOUT

*Tell me again, please, what is benchmarking?...
Lessons from Sam Walton...How do I use these
ideas?...Why allocated time for benchmarking?...
Illustrations of successful knowledge re-use...Do
you really use total cost of ownership as
a tool?...They really should be called rare
practices...Benchmarking and supply management.*

Tell me again, please, what is benchmarking?

Benchmarking is unusual in that it is a relatively new buzz-word that hasn't died after one or two years. It has spawned the term best practice, which is more explanatory.

The term, benchmarking, sounds like something you do to inanimate objects, such as comparing the speed of one computer against another. In actuality—

• It is a process rather than a program or system such as MRP or ERP.

• It is a process that requires a systematic approach applied continuously. It isn't a static ratio or an average performance level contrasted to your primary competitors.

• It is a means for effectively evaluating an organization's work methods and processes, its service products, and manufactured products against a meaningful best practice.

• Effective benchmarking requires that you consistently measure yourself against organizations that are successful illustrations for a specific process or method, etc.

• The process or method should be important (e.g. supplier quality in parts per million). Who cares how many requisitions one of your buyers processes per day? Clerical averages aren't worth much.

• The purpose of the benchmarking process in your department should be to uncover good ideas and take appropriate action(s) to improve the performance of your organization.

Lessons from Sam Walton

Sam Walton went from debtor with one heavily-mortgaged store to billionaire and largest retailer in the world. He did it on the strength of his personal dedication to learning from others.

Sam's personal process for what I like to call Continuous Comparison was a combination of reverse engineering, competitive analysis, and benchmarking! Many people are confused on the applications of these tools for continuous improvement:

• Reverse engineering generally applies to manufactured products, but Sam Walton applied it to merchandising operations. Over 30 years ago he traveled on an overnight bus from Arkansas to Minnesota to visit two prototype stores he read about. He spent the entire day reverse-engineering them, sketching layouts and taking notes on such things as size and construction of store fixtures. He went on to build thousands of stores based on ideas generated by this trip and subsequent visits to other sources of good ideas.

• Competitive analysis generally applies to market, product functions, and services. Walton's children fondly remember that he couldn't drive past a Kmart without stopping. He learned to fly a plane so he could conduct a great deal of competitive analysis.

When he flew over a town, he habitually flew over Kmart and counted the cars in the parking lot. After landing he had at least one valid business indicator to review with associates.

• Benchmarking applies to products, processes, and functions. Walton successfully built the world's largest discount operation around his many trips to learn from others with more expertise in core processes: buying, warehousing, transporting, merchandising. As a result, I believe he strategically set out to build core competencies in these processes: low cost distribution (including cross docking), supplier management, strategic management information services, and employee relations.

Today Wal-Mart has annual sales near $120 billion. Many ex-merchants do not share my appreciation of Walton's leadershuip and managerial skills. If they had been avid readers and if they had been willing to ride overnight buses to learn from others, they might still be in business. Walton focused on winning by providing customers with best value—always. His company has succeeded rather well—so far.

How do I use these ideas?

I would like to bring a 30,000 ft. idea down to earth for some practical review. The idea is that purchasing can be a core competence for a company.

If core competence is not a familiar term, I will elaborate as follows: True core competencies are few and not easily or quickly emulated or surpassed by your best competitors.

Core competencies also provide considerable value in the eyes of customers for your product or service. They are a unique capability that can generate long-term success and they are able to support multiple products and services. Conversely, a product or service can contain more than one core competence.

Some examples:

• Wal-Mart in strategic information systems and low-cost distribution that includes how they manage supply and suppliers.

• Honda in design and manufacture of small engines and power trains for a wide variety of products. Honda's creative supplier relationships have suported the evolution from small scooters to a wide variety of motorized products.

You may be asking: Where should I start at my company and how can continuous comparison or benchmarking help?

The process starts in your company, particularly if you have multiple locations, divisions, focused-factories, etc. I say this because many internal best practices can be located if you look for them. Knowledge re-use is a very powerful way to gain rapid progress with minimal resources and cost. For years, I have done this process looking for low hanging fruit to pick and enjoy.

Looking inside should lead to some internal baselines of current performance. This is very important so that you have a credible gauge for measuring future progress. This will require developing and using a few common measures that are the foundation for internal comparisons and will quickly speed the re-use of successful processes. Being good at using measures to derive more rapid progress is a rare competence.

Why allocate time for benchmarking?

Today most of our readers deal with these issues: increasing pressures to provide products and services to customers more rapidly, more flexibility with higher quality, and with greater economic results. In addition, they must operate with fewer internal resources than they have and/or feel they need. The good news is that many U.S. companies are doing well in this new world and are good candidates for benchmarking.

A common definition of insanity is "expecting major improvements while doing things the same old way." And when we look at the new things successful companies have learned, one truth stands out: The functional or command and control organizational structure frequently is not capable of responding quickly and effectively to today's market demands. Another is the need to improve processes so the business becomes capable of consistently satisfying its customers.

Such introspective analysis has led a growing number of companies to discover that they have paid inadequate attention to the procurement process. Frequently, they find this process does not really have an owner. Often, the paperwork is shuffled to someone in purchasing who documents the transactions, but who is not allowed to add much measurable value.

Many senior executives are beginning to discover that the procurement process and how supply is managed can be of strategic importance in the future of their business. It follows, therefore, that in many companies today there is a great opportunity for a supply management professional to be recognized and rewarded as a more valuable member of the team. However, these professionals are liable to miss the brass ring if they are perceived to be part of the problem rather than part of the solution.

To change that perception, purchasing pros need to allocate time to benchmarking. Yes, it does require a higher priority on how time is allocated. But a growing number of professionals are making the change. To illustrate: Last night, I and approximately 150 others attended a dinner meeting of a professional society. The topic was a case study in transforming a global supply chain. The speaker was the executive leader of the process. He candidly shared the good, bad, and ugly. Attendees gained an excellent insight into the project, the supporting resources, costs, reasons for success, and critical success factors.

Illustrations of successful knowledge re-use

The term—benchmarking—does not easily lead to a common, accurate understanding of its value. Personally, I prefer such terms as "continuous comparison for the purpose of knowledge re-use." We're looking for ways to enable organizations to improve quickly at modest expense. Re-using good ideas, practices, processes, etc., is not an end but a means to accelerate the rate of change in an organization so the organization can increase the pace of change in the future.

Learning from others is a trait that is common in our youth, but still often withers as we become adults. My six year old grandson Philip, for instance, carefully studies and emulates the best practices of his idols, such as Michael Jordan, his father, his soccer coach. His personal benchmark last season was 11 goals and the team won all but one game. Knowledge and process re-use should also help you win.

But it isn't all that simple. Today, for example, there is a continuing stream of expenses related to customer-mandated quality programs such as ISO 9000 and QS 9000. Unfortunately, it appears the compliance costs for most organizations is significantly greater than benefits gained from these programs.

So, you may ask, is there a better process we should study as a more cost effective approach? One place worth trying is the computer industry. It operates in a highly competitive, fast paced, progressive, global environment. Most of the industry leaders have formed CIQC (the Computer Industry Quality Conference). It's mission is "to promote a common focus and continuous improvement in electronic component quality and the practices used to purchase and deliver these products." CIQC members buy more than $12 billion of electronic components so CIQC influence is significant, as the active member companies recognize a common need to continuously improve supplier quality and business practices. The primary output of this collaboration is a growing list of common standards that make it easier and less costly for computer industry suppliers to cope with customer requirements. Standards make much more economic sense than a mandated, expensive audit focused on procedures.

Making quality improvements easier and less costly makes much more sense than today's most common customer quality initiatives.

Readers seriously concerned with quality improvement should benchmark the CIQC and consider re-using its valuable contributions.

Sometimes, too, the best practices are so obvious we tend to pass them by. For instance, a consulting client recently asked me for advice on where a team from his company should go to observe the best practices in receiving. I suggested the team visit the local supermarket to watch the best practices of bread suppliers. The bread suppliers arrive unsupervised, evaluate near-term sales by SKU, remove aging product, put a new product mix on the shelf, etc. The supermarket expends minimum resources on receiving because it trusts the supplier to do the process properly.

Do you really use total cost of ownership as a tool?

Several people have recently expressed dismay at how often benchmarking studies are equated with price comparisons. Sometimes, they note, the word "cost" is used, but after some additional conversation, it quickly becomes apparent that the other parties are really fixated on price as the important benchmark attribute. All of this begs two very important questions:

• How does your organization rate the importance of price comparison information?

• What priority does it have in our dealings with suppliers?

•Over the years much has been said and written about optimizing the procurement process via more attention to total cost of ownership or similar terms. But does your organization really use total cost of ownership as an important tool? Does it do so consistently? If not, is price still the prevailing measure? And is persuading suppliers to make large price concessions a primary goal?

Is it true that hard-to-measure cost elements deserve greater attention? Frequently I think they do. Often I think such measures deserve an appropriate benchmarking study.

Often I see businesses that claim they are forced to establish high selling prices as the result of ineffective purchasing, which allows their suppliers to sell to them at excessive prices. Such firms are not fun places to work for purchasing managers. Marketing and engineering have the primary influences in product offerings that are then tossed over the wall to purchasing and manufacturing. When I enquire in such firms about processes such as design for procurement or design for supply chain/postponement, both marketing and engineering functions usually demonstrate a lack of familarity with these important processes.

Let's look a little further at the powerful benefits of focusing on product offerings and the process of trying to get more out of less. To illustrate, Compaq has been taking market share away from IBM in PCs and servers for some time. For most of the past decade financial gurus have been highly critical of IBM and its poor financial performance in PCs. But, did any one notice that in 1998 IBM became more effective in supply management and has taken market leadership from Compaq? In a recent interview IBM revealed that it has cut costs and complexity in PCs by the following actions since 1994:

- Reducing the number of models assembled in IBM plants from 3400 to 150.

- Increasing the percentage of PCs assembled by distributors from 0% to 31%.

- Reducing available options from 750 to 350.

- Reducing major component types from 400 to 200.

- Reducing the number of parts carried in inventory from 56,000 to 15,000.

- Increasing parts replenished daily by suppliers from 5% to 62%.

- Reducing IBM employment by 7.5%,

What this seems to tell me is that IBM management understands design for procurement and design for supply/postponement. Compaq, on the other hand, may have overlooked Big Blue by being too focused on Dell. This is why benchmarking must be an ongoing process.

They really should be called rare practices

Benchmarking, as you know, is a continuous process for searching out the very best processes, tools, methods, etc., from successful companies, irrespective of your industry. When you restrict your search to your industry, then you are doing competitive analysis or reverse engineering. These better ways of doing things are broadly referred to as "best practices."

Best practices may not be the very best term to use. In my opinion they should be called "rare practices" because they generally have not been adopted by most organizations. Much has been written and said over the years about some rare practices, but many purchasing departments haven't adopted them. Possibly the "not invented here syndrome," and "our business is different" philosophy are perennials, like crabgrass in your lawn every summer.

I have concluded that the rare use of these foreign or "best" concepts is to blame. "Why should I take a risk implementing a rare practice? Things may go wrong and I might be blamed and lose my job."

Frequently I have used the term continuous comparison in lieu of benchmarking. I strongly recommend that conservative, slower to innovate organizations should be comparing where they are against "good" and "better" practices that are more broadly in use in successful organizations. Don't sweat "rare" and "best" when you still haven't gotten around to "good" and "better."

In the limited space remaining, let's have a brief test. Please score your organization on its use of the following "good" and "better" practices:

• We have written strategies in use for managing supply in our most important supply or commodity markets. Our strategies are part of our overall strategic plan.

• Approximately 25 suppliers represent approximately 80% of our annual spend. We devote 80% of our resources to these relationships, including quarterly senior executive reviews from both buyer and seller organizations.

• Procurement cards and integrated supply are widely and successfully implemented, enabling heavy resource concentration on important procurements.

• Your major suppliers receive a maximum of one purchase order per year. Transactions are accomplished electronically and/or by supplier personnel residing in your organization.

• The supplier manages your inventory freeing up your resources to work on strategic issues.

• You have a "credible" preferred supplier list that is the foundation for future sourcing decisions. Engineering no longer is the real sourcing department.

• A successful supplier advisory board has been successfully implemented.

• You are acting upon resolving deficiencies uncovered by a confidential supplier satisfaction survey.

If you didn't score 100, you need to spend more time and priority on benchmarking and continuous comparison.

Benchmarking and supply management

Is it feasible in your organization to look at supply management as a major source of future profits? Why not? If you benchmark leading companies such as Dell, Wal-Mart, Honda, Cisco, Chrysler, Sun Microsystems, and Solectron, you should be aware that their above average historical and current profitability is heavily impacted by how they manage their major markets and supplier relationships.

Is the current level of management interest in supply management a current fad that will be short-lived or is this a permanent elevation of supply considerations to the boardroom for strategic review? Benchmarking, it seems to me, may be that one tool that can help companies make that evaluation.

In the late 1960s, as I recall, there was a similar rush of management interest in a new concept that offered significant potential benefits—materials management. I remember reading an excellent article by an industry expert, Dean Ammer, who predicted that materials management would become a profit center in many companies and industries. His forecast foretold that the new corporate materials managers would become vice presidents, their functions would be elevated to parity with sales, finance, and manufacturing. This is finally happening today in a number of companies and organizations, but it is also obvious that in most companies Dean Ammer's forecast never came about.

It is fair to ask why, and whether any of the past problems still have some potential today to derail the growing supply management momentum. I've done some benchmarking and analysis on what the barriers and root causes were that widely impacted materials management.

Problems started with the basic approach to materials management. It called for the creation of a new functional silo—materials management. Few companies went much beyond that. Fewer still, were the successes of companies in using multi-functional teams to effectively manage flows of materials.

People were selected and promoted based on perceived <u>management</u> skills—professional certifications from NAPM and APICS, etc. <u>Leadership</u> skills directed at <u>process</u> improvement got short shrift.

It was rare for companies to take a <u>holistic</u> approach to managing materials. Key measures and systems were, in most cases, inwardly focused. Few individuals and organizations were concerned or focused on chains of suppliers for their products. In short, a strategic approach to materials was uncommon.

Reach out or stretch goals were rarely put in place to generate out-of-the-box thinking. If goals are conventional, you typically get conventional approaches to improvements. The wisdom of the goals set by people like Michael Dell and Sam Walton was not readily apparent—until recently.

Conventional solutions were widely adopted, e.g. computer

systems such as MRP and MRP II. Eli Goldratt and his OPT software were widely reviewed. The vested interests in technical solutions fought long battles with proponents of common sense approaches, such as JIT and lean manufacturing.

The most common MRP and MRP II software, for many years, did not contain effective means to support the process of purchasing and managing suppliers. That's still true today in many companies.

Most organizations were overly focused on their internal operations and had inadequate focus, processes, and resources to manage supplier and customer linkages and relationships.

Inappropriate financial information was widely used in decision making and many many bad decisions were made that may be very difficult to reverse or correct quickly.

Perhaps most important lesson that can be learned from this look at material management's disappointing performance is that very little benchmarking was done as a means of sharing best materials management practices.

Section 3

THE SMELL OF SUCCESS

There's nothing like a well-conceived plan... Information analysis...Integration: Beware management's denial phase...Action phase: Benchmarking's critical success factor...What to benchmark...The value of choosing to be different... Linking educaiton and training with benchmarking...Good ideas never die, Learning from others.

There's nothing like a well-conceived plan

Benchmarking is essentially a four-step process consisting of planning, analysis, integration, and action. Today we will concentrate on planning. Every benchmarking effort must start with a well-conceived—and well executed—plan.

But remember, analysis is the second in our four-step process. Many efforts derail early because a plan doesn't provide for effective analysis of comparisons with benchmarking partners.

Keep in mind that obvious benchmarking candidates are also obvious to others. Leading firms may think of benchmarking as a curse and are likely to have erected effective barriers to prevent access by amateurs. Indeed, many would-be benchmarkers are unable to gain access to leading companies because it is obvious they don't understand the benchmarking process. One solution is a well conceived plan, attractively presented in terms of how the host company will benefit.

A good plan for continuous comparison should specify what is to be benchmarked. Some ideas that come to mind:

• Measure annual price changes in total as a percent of total use.

• Evaluate results attained by corporations that use total cost of ownership for sourcing future business.

• Determine how senior executives in leading corporations measure the effectiveness of their purchasing, strategic sourcing, or supply management functions.

• Determine what functions (in leading corporations) have significant influence in strategic sourcing decisions; benchmark against their historical improvement in quality, delivery, and cost.

Who should benchmark? This is of major importance. Sam Walton spent his life doing it—so should your CEO, his staff, your boss, and you. For a minute, imagine you're leading a benchmarking visit to a company that does wonderful things, has great results, and is charging full speed ahead. They may be 5-10 years ahead of your company, thanks to superior management. What will your trip report look like? Will your job security be diminished if your team's report is realistic and clues in management on the need to eliminate unfavorable variance? A visit such as I describe should be a religious experience for the relevant senior executives of your company.

Finally, how will the data be collected? Start with other departments in your company that may have already collected considerable data and meaningful analysis on the companies you are targeting. Before you consider asking for access to the target companies, legitimately and ethically work the following public domains: libraries, databases, professional associations, suppliers, customers, annual reports, and consultants.

Information analysis

The analysis step is most successful when the prior planning phase has been focused on reviewing the strategic direction of a benchmarking partner and when a partner's strategies are comparable with our situation. It's also a good learning tool if we succeed in answering these questions:

- Is someone outperforming us?
- Why is their performance better?
- How are they doing it?
- What can we learn by analyzing their approach versus ours?
- How can we apply what we have learned?
- If our performance is better in some respects, how can we stay ahead or widen our lead?

I remember a well executed study of six leading firms and the specific strategies used by each. Two had been awarded Purchasing Magazine's annual Medal of Professional Excellence award. Three had earned Malcolm Baldrige National Quality Awards. all six firms were involved in highly competitive industries. The team found tremendous similarities among the six benchmarking hosts; in fact, it found consensus use of these procurement strategies:

- Pooled purchase agreements.
- Strategic commodity plans.
- Global sourcing strategy.
- Process benchmarking.
- Supplier design involvement.

• Statistical process control.

Unfortunately, not all six had remained prosperous. Some had fallen on hard times. Others returned to prosperity from hard times. One—a Japanese firm—had begun with a clean-sheet approach and avoided the roller coaster rides of the others. Of the three doing well in tough markets, two additional strategies were observed.

• A common vision clearly spelled out, across the entire corporation. Purchasing and sourcing strategies were appropriate to the strategic direction of the business.

• Design guidelines had been developed—with aid from suppliers. The guides were being used in the design function.

These two uncommon strategies are the foundation of the competitive strengths that answer these questions:

• Why is their performance better than ours?

• How are they doing it?

• What can we learn by analyzing their approach versus ours?

• How can we apply what we have learned?

Integration:
Beware management's denial phase

Integration is the third step in our presentation of a four-step continuous comparison (benchmarking) process (see chart on page 42). Key issues that can arise after thorough information analysis are:

• Has or will management accept or buy-in to our findings and recommendations? Too often executives go very quickly into denial—"No one can be that much better than us. Your data must be wrong!"

• Is there a need to change goals and objectives? Again, denial can arise quickly—"Your data is wrong. If it were possible to reduce product costs by 25% per year, we'd already have done it ourselves."

• Have new goals been clearly communicated (or will they be communicated) to all organizations involved? This also entails developing appropriate strategies and new operating plans and goals.

When Motorola management communicated its Six Sigma goal several years ago it initially engendered some disbelief: "They want us to improve 68% per year, compounded?!" The new goal was based on a thorough, well executed comparison of quality performance. Senior management bought into the comparison results, the findings were integrated into a set of "reach out" goals, and the rest is history.

Caution: Cause and effect is not always as straightforward as it would seem. You need to keep asking Why? until you get to the true cause. To illustrate, a multi-company study was made of materials management overhead rates as a percent of material purchased. Purchasing departments in some companies had overhead cost structures that were 50% greater than the norm. (Look out, here come outside reengineers!). Remaining segments of the materials management overhead structures in some companies were nearly double the norm. (Look out, another project for the outside reengineering crusade!)

Any guesses on root causes? Informnation technology is the oft prescribed reengineering solution. It was also the root of much greater than average overhead costs. These companies were pursuing fervently Class A MRP or MRP II status prescribed by the gurus of that era. Their overly complex systems required overly large staffs to deal with systems outputs, for example, exception messages. Ultimate solution was not more smart systems. Rather, the study reinforced a belief that a simple system used effectively by a few smart people was the low cost solution. This is why detectives like Perry Mason and Columbo became highly respected for their investigative skills.

Action phase:
Benchmarking's critical success factor

A good friend recently commented to me on the importance of involving senior executives in the planning phase so it won't be such a big surprise when the results become available. Senior executives need to be appropriately involved in all four steps: planning, analysis, integration, and action.

The action phase is basically very straight-forward. Ask these questions:

• Have we identified the work steps necesasary to achieve our goals?

• Are we tracking progress to our goals?

• What is our plan to recalibrate to determine if our rate of change is still appropriate?

To illustrate, I recently spoke with an executive in a company that has made major improvements in quality, cost, and market share over the past 10 years. More recently, it has been burdened with hosting many prospective benchmarkers.

This company recently discovered that it is no longer a low cost producer. A smaller company, using some unconventional practices involving collaboration with its supply base, has suddenly emerged as the low cost producer. In addition to racking up larger profits, it also is grabbinbg market share. Its purchasing director is now besieged by prospective benchmarkers.

The purchasing function is naturally in the spotlight. Objective analysis shows that better design involving suppliers and purchasing was the major reason for the competitor's unexpected success. Senior management is now causing major organizational changes. If the company had seen benchmarking on continuous comparison as an ongoing process it would have remained in the lead.

The former leader has several alternatives in its plan to close the competitive gap:

• **It can try harder.** This is the easiest choice, but it is unlikely to result in the company regaining its former leadership role.

• **It can emulate.** This is a good choice because the company can benefit quickly by employing the processes successfully used by a competitor. However, stopping with this step dooms the company to a follower status.

• **It can leapfrog.** In addition to emulation, leapfrogging can lead to regaining the company's former leadership role. Leapfrog is what the competition did to it.

• **It can change the rules of the game.** In Section 2 we illustrated how Sam Walton did this very successfully.

What to benchmark

How do you make benchmarking provide your organization with improved results quickly? Start by identifying the few things the organization must do well to effectively compete and prosper versus competitors. In essence, it is necessary to identify:

• Core competencies.

• Critical success factors.

• Strategic success factors.

Don't waste time trying to benchmark prior to understanding these strategic issues. They are the key processes that create satisfied customers and job security for your employees and your suppliers.

To illustrate, let's turn to Sam Walton. In his book, *Made in America, My Story*, Walton spells out these rules for success:

1. Commit to your business. Believe in it more than anyone else.

2. Share your profits with all your associates, and treat them as partners. In turn, they will treat you as a partner, and together you will all perform beyond your wildest expectations.

3. Motivate your partners. Money and ownership aren't enough. Constantly, day by day, think of new and more interesting ways to motivate and change your partners. Set high goals, encourage competition, and then keep score.

4. Communicate everything you possibly can to your partners. The more they know, the more they'll understand. The more they understand, the more they'll care. Once they care, there's no stopping them.

5. Appreciate everything your partners do for the business. All of us like to be told how much somebody appreciates what we do for them.

6. Celebrate your success. Find some humor in your failures.

7. Listen to everyone. Figure out ways to get them talking.

8. Exceed your customers' expectations. If you do, they'll come back over and over.

9. Control your expenses better than your competition. This is where you can always find the competitive advantage.

10. Swim upstream. Go the other way. Ignore the conventional wisdom.

Which of Sam Walton's rules—if dilligently applied to your organization—will create core competence and competitive advantage for your company?

The value of choosing to be different

I like the advice of the great philosopher Yogi Berra: "When you come to a fork in the road, take it." Many readers are at a fork in the process of continuous comparison.

Conventional wisdom places a heavy focus on numerical averages and other quantifiable data related to costs for activities commonly performed in your function and/or industry. For example: number of purchase orders placed per buyer, average direct labor hours per unit produced, etc. But if you and your competitors are all hard at work improving the same activities to achieve a common performance norm, your competitive positions will be affected.

Today, supply chain management is an area of great interest, focus, and hightened activity. Major changes are taking place and large sums of money are changing hands quickly due to huge budgets for software and implementation of enterprise resource planning. Outsourcing of the logistics function to a third party provider is also a very popular change today. But, if you and your major competitors are purchasing the same software and logistics suppliers, your competitive positions will not change. Unless you successfully differentiate yourself in a way that benefits your customers in a significant way.

I am amazed at how few people ever ask me, "Who is world class in relationship management with their strategic suppliers?" It implies to me that they believe this isn't important.

Suppliers tend to have needs and wants, just like your company. Customers who are genuinely interested in relationships that also benefit their suppliers typically receive economic benefits from preferential treatment. Becoming good at relational management requires a process focus, a process owner, long-term commitment, tools and measures, and goals. I typically see programs, such as the current stampede for outsourcing, not processes. The other fork or alternative is to benchmark effectively, to learn how to successfully outsource and manage the ongoing relationship.

Linking education and training with benchmarking

All too often executives fail to appreciate the important role that education and training can play in eliminating performance gaps uncovered in benchmarking best practice organizations.

Performance gaps can be narrowed, and possibly eliminated by successfully trying harder, emulating best practices of others, leapfrogging, and changing the rules of the game. Sam Walton, founder of Wal-Mart, is a superb example of a small entrepreneur who consistently learned from studying his competition and then leading his organization to become the largest retailer in the world. He didn't go to academia to find role models.

Among other organizations that have made great progress, part of their strategy is to upgrade their employees' understanding of best practices (education) and transfer knowledge on how to apply the lessons learned in their business (training). Over the years I have found it very beneficial to seek out external experts and to have them deliver customized educational or training courses for my people. The application of lessons learned can be accelerated into a common learning experience for the entire staff at one time. Frequently this approach acts as a starting point to which people can refer as they take personal ownership for new ways and processes.

It is not easy to create change or to reduce a performance gap in supply management. Trying harder isn't the answer. Emulating a best practice can begin to show results and create an atmosphere that is receptive to new ideas, but you are still behind someone else. It is necessary to expose people to experts who can stimulate thought processes that leapfrog existing cost practices and competitors—better yet, that figure out how to change the rules of the game.

Finding and selecting an expert frequently isn't easy. It is like learning to swim. A prospective coach is first certified as a skilled swimmer prior to becoming swimming instructor. You need to be able to have your organization move across performance gaps, and not disappear halfway across.

Good ideas never die

In today's world of ever shorter life cycles and tidal waves of new buzzwords, it's easy to move away from valuable common sense solutions that still have their place in a successful process.

It is also very easy to get confused as to the real principles that underpin a change management tool, such as benchmarking. I tell people that the essence of benchmarking is constant comparison to something that is a best practice with the specific intent of knowledge re-use for the purpose of organizational improvement. A good friend, Tom Slaninka of Motorola, recently shared with me the following more comprehensive explanation:

1. Find, say, 10 or 15 individuals (preferably in a variety of businesses and geographic locations) who are especially skillful in the processes to be evaluated.

2. Study the exact series of steps that each uses in processes along with the tools and systems used.

3. Study and carefully measure the time required for each process

step and then select the easiest way to perform each activity.

4. Eliminate all activities that are slow and not useful.

5. Build into your process the quickest and best process steps and the best tools.

The advice he shared with me is nearly 100 years old and comes from Frederick W. Taylor, the father of scientific management. If we change a few words to current technology, it seems very contemporary. Taylor's work generated incredible improvements in productivity. If you haven't done a good benchmarking study recently, now may be a good time to start.

Learning from others

An early benefit of the benchmarking process should be forming a regular habit of continuously comparing your performance in a particular area against other organizations. Most managers like to know how well they compare to someone else they respect.

Given the major progress in decentralization in prior years, I am amazed that few heavily decentralized companies still have functional peer reviews performed regularly to transfer internal best practices to other locations. An additional reason for these reviews is to access (benchmark) performance levels on similar processes and functions in different organizations.

In any case, functional peer reviews used to be a common improvement tool in diversified corporations. A large electronics company, for instance, was very successful in developing an excellent quality performance program, and the cornerstone of its process was a functional peer review. The company started with a baseline of definitions of processes and tools, measures, etc., that should be used in an effective quality system. A team of five directors of quality from a variety of businesses would spend a few days auditing, in depth, the quality system of another division. The baseline process resulted in a numerical score and a large number of suggestions of things the auditors had successfully used themselves and that were viewed as relevant to the host operation. The team would present its important findings to the general manager of the host operation.

Participating in functional peer reviews was not optional, but a priority in the eyes of senior management. In fact, quality improvement progress was a very high priority, even over profitability. Their businesses hosted quality reviews every two years, and if improvement wasn't apparent in the survey scores, the host general manager's career was in jeopardy. The parent corporation achieved huge reductions in the cost of quality.

Functional peer review is a great idea, like many others, that has declined in use over the years. Supply chain management is a high priority in many companies, and vast sums of money, time, and resources are being expended. In my opinion, it is an area that would greatly benefit from a functional peer review process. It requires developing a definition of what elements, processes, tools, measures, etc., should be in place in an effective supply management system. It is a reasonable expectation to have a roadmap in key areas such as planning, sourcing, purchasing processes, supplier development processes, supplier quality management, etc.

In a past life a few of us in a company developed a functional peer review in supply management. It represented a baseline of what was an effective system. Many great observations and recommendations were made by the auditors and presented to the host business.

A key output was a score and methodology that showed how good that operation was performing against a baseline.

BENCHMARKING
Closing the Gap

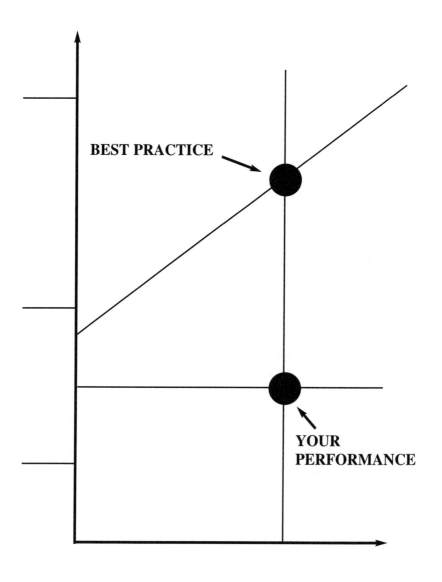

Section 4

WORDS OF WISDOM FROM ACTIVE PROGRAMS

Selecting a proper project...Lessons from the Japanese...Knowledge re-use award...Knowledge re-use revisited...Hello—I'm here to audit your books...Size is no deterrent...Even the best can fall on their faces...How good is your timing?...Be careful about who you tell about your best practice.

Selecting a proper project

Our objective today is to share some ideas on how to select a useful benchmarking project in a process of effective continuous improvement.

A by-product of reengineering projects has been a grading of purchasing departments—like commodities—into broad categories:

- 80% reactive fire fighters.
- 15% proactive, fire prevention.
- 5% strategic orientation.

Many of us rose through the management ranks by virtue of our skills and involvement in solving daily crises. As a result, boredom comes quickly if we make considerable progress with our strategic sourcing and supplier management initiatives, causing our crisis management skills to atrophy.

Most business executives err by not involving their purchasing managers in their strategy development processes. Consequently, only 5% or so are graded "strategically oriented."

How do we change this chicken and egg scenario? Benchmarking our cost per purchase order and the average number of requisitions processed annually per buyer in our SIC code is more likely to further scramble management's assessment of our value. However, a process that leads to a valid comparison—not on efficiency, but effectiveness—could be very beneficial. In fact, senior executives frequently ask me variations on these questions

• What kinds of annual results are turned in by companies that are recognized for being world class at managing supply?

• How do we compare?

• What should we do to be like them—soon?

What are the major questions your management asks? There is at least one good benchmarking project here.

Lessons from the Japanese

Tremendous progress logged by Japanese companies after World War II is strong testimony to the power of benchmarking or continuous comparison. Here's what happens in a typical Japanese process:

1. Senior management of Japanese companies willingly authorize considerable expenditures to visit and analyze work practices at other companies. Top managers realize these so-called costs are effective investments needed to foster competitiveness. They wish to quickly emulate best practices.

2. The Japanese have a specific plan for each trip—they plan topics to study, what to look into, who is a good candidate for a productive visit, etc. Visiting teams represent functions that would most benefit from the visit. And the best people are sent—not

those who can be spared!

3. Detailed, comprehensive questions are developed in advance. Teams gather data to answer their own questions. When they stumble on excellent performance representing a best practice, they can focus on gaining a deeper understanding of the reasons for superior performance.

4. Japanese firms have a bias for action. Knowledge, processes, and practices are adopted and re-used. (A typical American team writes reports and files them away, benefiting only file-cabinet makers, airlines, hotels, and car rental companies.)

5. Japanese firms look outside their own industries for good ideas. American supermarkets, for instance, were the inspiration for the kanban replenishment system. Side-loading American beverage trucks are widely used in Japan for all types of industries.

6. Japanese firms follow a continuous process. It isn't just a program of the year.

7. Japanese continuously refine the data gathering, comparison process. Kaizen always makes sense.

Knowledge Re-Use Award

Former President Reagan was in office when the Malcolm Baldrige Nation Quality Award competition was initiated in 1987.

If, by magic or other miraculous circumstance, I were to become President, my first official act would be to commission the National Knowledge Re-Use Award competition. Unlike the Baldrige, it would not restrict the prize to a maximum of six winners. More is definitely better.

Knowledge re-use deserves a very high priority in American business. In my career, I have continually seen well-meaning, talented people designing unique solutions when uniqueness was not called for by the customer. Common byproducts of such activities were parts nearly impossible to make; new, not yet capable processes requiring development; expensive qualifications of new, unproven suppliers. Cost overruns and delays in production were not unknown.

Money and time spent would have been less if there were equal and opposite influences in place to consider knowledge re-use.

American corporations are making progress in this area: Concurrent product development is now in vogue. So is design for manufacturability and design for assembly. Too few companies pursue an objective that my friend Barry Hawking of Ingersoll-Rand calls design for procurement. Simply stated, instead of start ing out with a blank sheet of paper, why not use common or standard parts, a proven technology, an historically great supplier?

Many businesses are reengineering the procurement process— frequently because the company has far too many suppliers, buyers, quality problems, and high costs.

If we create the Natiuonal Knowledge Re-Use Award, we might be able to significantly increase the time span between procurement process reengineering projects in America!

Knowledge re-use revisited

Recently I listened to a presentation on the results of a reengineering project at a large consumer products company. It was touted as a best-practice operation to be emulated. Among its accomplishments was elimination of thousands of suppliers and a majority of purchasing employees, and a savings of more than $100 million. Should a global manufacturer of engineered products re-use such knowledge, or is there a better model of success?

One industry source shows that in a particular industry, total purchasing headcount represents less than 1% of total employment, each person in purchasing supports $8.5 million worth of purchases, so on and so forth. This source does not concern itself with quality or service performance of suppliers in the industry. Should it? And can this data help us set future goals?

In contrast, let's look at some data from Honda of America Manufacturing—a company with a remarkably loyal customer base—for the year 1994. The numbers were supplied by Dave Nelson, former VP of purchasing. In 1994, Honda had approximately 320 North American suppliers and approximately 300 people in the purchasing department. In other words, this ratio of buyers to suppliers was approximately one to one. Honda also had 200 parts quality engineers and 300 other engineers available to help its 320 suppliers. All 800 resources were available to provide hands-on support, in the supplier's plant when needed to improve quality, delivery, cost, productivity, etc.

To quote Nelson, "We have much more information on what things do and should cost than we have resources." Best practice at Honda is called "supplier development process." It should be better understood, because it's one of Honda's critical success factors. In many companies, reengineering programs have caused dramatic reductions in purchasing staff and budget. Meanwhile, the Honda team of 800 and its 320 suppliers continue to please customers, and it seems that this is what best practice should be about.

Hello—I'm here to audit your books

In our last column we reviewed some of the excellent proceses and resources used by Dave Nelson, former vice president of purchasing for Honda America Manufacturing.

In my opinion, Dave and his team achieved some remarkable results because they had a long-term management commitment to helping their suppliers become world class on quality, productivity, and cost. The general term for this type of program is supplier development.

For a frame of reference, approximnately 40% of Honda's purchasing staff are devoted to long-term strategic activities and the balance to daily (tactical) operations. Approximately 7% of United States employees are devoted to supply chain management and working toward continuous improvements in quality, delivery, productivity, and ultimately lowest total cost.

The opposite of Nelson's proactive approach is found in this example: Recently the president of a large company that supplies equipment to the energy industry called. He said that his largest customer—a giant multinational energy corporation—had launched a program aimed at finding ways to improve supply chain management. Now, as a requirement of doing business with it, the company is demanding full access to the cost systems of its suppliers.

Going no further than this much information, one is already led to surmise that this desire to send in the cost accountants is not directed at improving quality and delivery. Instead of sending in highly-qualified production experts to help solve vexing production problems, this customer appears to be positioning itself to tell suppliers they are paying janitors too much per hour and that the housekeeping expenses are beyond their reinbursement policy.

Clearly this approach does not require 40% of the purchasing staff to be strategic. A modicum of expertise in reading financial statements is the major need. I hope the energy company some day learns about Honda's approach because I am a customer, and I think its finance staff is too large.

Size is no deterrent

Frequently I hear executives at small and medium-sized companies say they don't do much benchmarking. They offer a wide variety of excuses, most commonly: "We're too small, we don't have the time and resources, benchmarking is for big companies..."

My response is to tell the story of a small businessman who was struggling to survive against intense local competition. He had a large bank loan that was a frequent concern, given the small profit margin in his industry. He aspired to expand his business so he could provide jobs to family members.

The small enterpreneur read an article in a publication about two businesses that were possibly employing some new business concepts. They were in a distant state. The owner lacked someone to send, but he was a proactive individual, curious and intrigued by the story he read. So he delegated himself, and traveled by overnight bus to the distant location he read about.

He spent an entire day studying in very great detail the two locations he read about. He did benchmarking. He did competitive analysis and he did some reverse engineering. At the end of the day he got on another overnight bus and returned home.

The entrepreneur had tons of notes on a yellow legal pad that he studied very carefully. He had no boss waiting for a trip report. He merely began to carefully implement in his business the new ideas he picked up on his benchmarking trip.

His business began to improve and he attributed some of its new success to lessons learned from the people and businesses he had studied.

He allocated more of his valuable executive time to making more trips to learn from others. Eventually this grew to four days per week visiting others. Then he learned to fly a plane so he could visit more places each week.

The entrepreneur had always been interested in the purchase of the items his company resold. He wanted to be the low cost alternative in the marketplace. He also wanted to make a fair profit so he could expand his business.

He and his associates developed some unique approaches and processes (best practices) in his procurement and logistics operations. In essence they developed a well planned strategy on how to succeed in an industry of high supplier commonality.

Meanwhile, executives at the large companies he began to compete against remained busy as usual—too busy to spend time, much less four days a week, learning from others.

The entrepreneur, if you haven't already guessed, was Sam Walton. Over a roughly 30-year period his company grew from one small dime store in Arkansas to over 3000 stores and $100 billion in sales. He became the largest retailer in the world, offering low prices, but enjoying well above-average profitability. Walton built a benchmark for others to study.

I used to tell Sam Walton tales to some Sears executives in our Friday night tennis league. I stopped when their jobs were eliminated.

Even the best can fall on their faces

Success can frequently be a terrible curse for any widely lauded organization. The curse of success, as I call it, can easily lead to complacency. And that pretty much sums up the situation of many Japanese and Asian banking firms these days.

For years I have cited Japanese manufacturers as an outstanding example of a huge success resulting from application of lessons learned on benchmarking visits to our country. They went to the very best people on specific missions and focused on learning best practices in specific areas.

Tokyo executives researched old Henry Ford's manufacturing processes. They added major refinements and small ones over the years while evolving their awesome Toyota production system frequently referred to as Just-In-Time.

Others mastered the concepts and intricacies of quality management. Effective benchmarking caused the Japanese quality students to ultimately surpass their American paradigms. In fact, not long ago, business publications were rife with epitaphs for American business. Many business magazines had cover stories foretelling the demise of Western capitalism and a world economy dominated by Asia. Western capitalism, as the story read, was no longer the best practice.

Unfortunately, while Japanese and other Asian bankers were reading their press notices, things were unraveling. Though they could have learned much from the American banking industry, which had gone through similar bad times, they failed to benchmark. They did not take the bitter corrective medecine required, and today the financial stability of Asia remains in trouble.

Complacency and other worst practices have resulted in a serious, deadly new disease that is now referred to as the Asian Flu. But, call it what you want, Asian leaders need to shed some of their cockiness and do some more serious benchmarking—this time of Western capitalism.

It's a reminder to all companies, that benchmarking is not only for those scrambling to reach the top; it's also important for those who want to stay on top.

Right now it's time for Japan and its Asian neighbors to put best practices in place. It's time for them to pull down "not invented here" barriers and return to some constructive benchmarking.

How good is your timing?

Employees at the Borg-Warner automotive plant in Frankfort, Ill., actively search for "BOBs" or "Best of the Best Practices". Their success in uncovering BOBs and appropriately using them to generate significant improvements resulted in a recent recognition and award for being one of America's best plants.

One of the best BOBs I ever came across was from Don Kasperek, 20 years ago. He was then a senior operations executive witha large, global, diversified operation. I met Don and learned of his BOB on a visit that today would be called benchmarking.

I had just joined a large corporation in a corporate staff position, a new one for the company and myself. In my prior position our president measured me on how quickly I evicted corporate staff from his 40 plants in 10 countries. Needless to say I had seen corporate staff as what I call today reverse benchmarks.

Don's advice or BOB was counter-intuitive in that he advised against developing and publishing a long-term strategy or financial plan.

His experience was that timing was always wrong—his report was read, considered, but not acted upon by senior management.

Later, when a business cycle dip occurred, Don would elevate his prior recommendations, but they would invariably be rejected as old ideas. Fresh ideas were demanded.

I generally followed Don's advice, which included drafting long-range strategies, but keeping them locked up for frequent reference in case timing might be right for some or much of the private plan.

It worked quite well. The vice-president once asked for a white paper on a subject of great interest to him. I volunteered and rather easily and quickly provided the white paper from materials I had been accumulating in anticipation of a future need. I got to present it to the board, it got approved and broadly supported, and lots of benefits were gained by the shareholders.

Later on, however, I violated Don's BOB and wrote another white paper before I was asked. The subject was so important, it couldn't wait—I thought. I wasted a lot of time and energy as the timing wasn't right.

Lots of BOBs are available from people like Don Kasperek who kindly share their wisdom with those just coming down the same path. In this age of tremendous change and new technologies, you should be careful to hear the common sense and advice of those with relevant experiences worth sharing.

Be careful who you tell about your best practice

An organization that has a best practice has a leg up on its competition. A good deal of time, effort, and money is required to create a best practice, particularly a new or unique best practice. But many times I'm surprised by how quickly the new best practice becomes public knowledge.

If I worked for a company that had developed a best practice, my preference would be to enjoy the economic benefits of lower costs, increased sales, etc. I'd be almost paranoid about keeping the best practice secret for a very good reason: I wouldn't want my competitors to find out what my company had accomplished. If they did, they quickly could emulate our hard-earned best practice.

People who are good at benchmarking typically possess superior networking skills. Personal relationships result from memberships in professional associations. Public seminars and conferences are common forums for acquiring in-depth knowledge of evolving best practices. But too many people share too much information too broadly on the latest and greatest best practices. I'm sure that most people share this type of information without reflecting on the possible repercussions, but that fact doesn't change the consequence of losing a competitive advantage.

I believe that benchmarking and exchanging information on best practices is great, but only when it's done on a mutually beneficial basis, with a benchmarking partner. To me, being a partner implies a private, confidential relationship where each party receives an in-depth understanding of the other party's processes, and respects the intellectual property rights of the other party. The benefits of such exchanges are restricted to only the partners.

My advice is this: Next time you develop or implement a best practice, be careful who you tell, or your advantage over your competitors may soon disappear.

Section 5

MISTAKES WAITING TO HAPPEN

Reverse benchmarks: A few observations on worst practices...Antoher look at reverse benchmarks... Yes, that may be true, but our business is different...Old mindsets may hinder success... Common bad benchmarking practices...Common benchmarking errors to avoid...Key negative factors to remember.

Reverse benchmarks:
A few observations on worst practices

In recent years many executives have shown new interest in how purchasing deals with suppliers. Frequently this interest is coupled with a belated realization that expenditures with suppliers represent more than 50% of sales dollars!

I strongly believe that the first step should be to see if the organization is guilty of any of the following outmoded behaviors (what I call worst practices):

• **Strategy.** Failing to link business strategies and objectives to the way in which critical procurements are managed on an on-going basis.

• **Reengineering.** Typically 80% of the current staff spends most of its time on small purchases. Automate and lay them off instead of re-focusing them on managing better the 80% of value that was historically under-managed.

• **Ethics.** Having a policy of frequent or annual rotation of buyers so that no one gets too close. This leads to a great many commitments made by inexperienced buyers.

• **Empowerment.** Failure to include procurement expertise on teams making major commitments.

• **Decentralization.** Everyone does his or her own thing in a company with multiline business. The shareholders of your suppliers appreciate this very much!

• **Education and training.** Expert advise is seen as expensive. What are the hidden costs of amateurs learning on the job?

• **Partnership.** A term we use freely without a common, well understood definition. For example, suppliers drop selling prices at least X percent per year. We raise our selling prices at every opportunity.

• **Win-win.** Similar to partnership, except a common score is : Customer 2, Suppliers 0.

• **Competing for supply.** Bad customers who practice the old, adversarial behaviors frequently suffer disruptions in supply. When Wall Street learns of it, suppliers get blamed for non-performance.

• **Forecasting.** To my knowledge, no company is good at forecasting sales. If they fail to effectively collaborate with critical suppliers on balancing supply and demand, then four classes of inventory occur—FIFO (first in, first out); LIFO (last in, first out); FISH (first in, still here); and OSWO (Oh S—, we're out!).

Another look at reverse benchmarks

This is a continuation of all too common behaviors that significantly and adversely affect the supply management process. Reflect on how your company operates as you read this:

1. Partnering. Expecting key suppliers to consistently meet the expectations of your firm. Meanwhile, the supplier frequently gets caught in the crossfire between some of your departments.

2. Quick response. Expecting key suppliers to consistently respond very rapidly. We are not attempting to be equally prompt when the supplier needs something from us.

3. Quality. Expectations for supplier performance are very high. Our expectations on quality performance internally are much lower. Our suppliers see this inconsistency.

4. Measurement. Our expectations of proper supplier performance change frequently. Measures of supplier performance are out of date and inappropriate.

5. Contracting. Your legal department exerts considerable energy in defining agreements with critical suppliers. Little time is spent on rewards for superior supplier performance. Considerable time spent on remedies if and when supplier fails to perform.

6. Outsourcing. Getting rid of non-critical activities without appropriate plans and resources to manage these new external supplier relationships. Very quickly users of the services from the new supplier experience a deterioration in performance. Who helps them when the buyers have been downsized also?

7. Design for procurement. No one knows what this means, or cares. Your major competitors appreciate this very much.

8. Accounts payable. We are a demanding customer but our accounting department takes 45 to 60 days to pay. Competitors who pay promptly receive preferential treatment while we nurse nickles on payables.

9. Supplier rating. Failing to frequently, consistently, fairly, and objectively provide feedback to key suppliers in progress to our expectations and how they rank against competitors.

10. Supply base management. Failing to recognize that this is a critical element in how you compete today. Companies that earn preferential treatment from their critical suppliers are already winning in the marketplace. They listen to the voice of their supplier and seek to be a world-class customer.

Yes, that may be true, but our business is different

We all have heard this comment countless times. I call it "the Skeetshooter's Lament." Skeetshooters are very common in most organizations. When a benchmarking team completes a study and presents its findings and recommendations, the skeetshooters attempt to kill all the good ideas so they won't have to change something, take a risk, or spend some money on investment. When all else fails, they then say, "We tried that before and it didn't work."

Recent columns have addressed worst practices that hobble the ability of business in today's competitive world. Skeetshooters belong in the Worst Practices Hall of Shame.

Another nomination is general managers who feel they are really good at prioritizing their time. They may allocate 15% to 20% of their time on customer issues. They travel frequently on customer visits with their senior sales and marketing executives. They have never visited a supplier and they allocate less than 5% of their time to supply management issues.

Then there are purchasing people who, unlike the sales and marketing types just cited, rarely seek senior management support on supply management issues. Often they fail to use external experts to provide expertise relevant to current problems.

Organizational reporting structures, despite all the reengineering hoopla, often are ripe for nomination to the Hall. Many are very slow to change at the top of an organization. Direct labor in many businesses today is well below 5% of sales, and still dropping. Often supply management costs are greater than 50% of sales and growing. Still, purchasing typically reports to the head of manufacturing, who continues to be paid a bonus based on labor productivity. Subordinates with job security help the boss make his goals.

In some industries there are signs of an economic slowdown. The classical cuts are being dusted off and implemented:

- Reduce travel to suppliers.
- Reduce education and training.
- Reduce reinbursement of memberships in professional societies.

The above activities are fertile areas for finding candidates. Not spending some expense money frequently prevents access to large savings.

Another nomination to the Worst Practices Hall of Shame is poor engineering standards. A frustrated supplier recently told a senior executive pursuing a further, large price concession, "Your company will be the last one on earth to use industry parts." The customer is the high cost producer in its industry and fails to grasp that its engineers are the primary cause.

Old mindsets may hinder success

Long held opinions and beliefs often have significant influence on benchmarking projects. Recently a consultant from a major firm tracked me down with the hope that I could answer an important question: "What is a current benchmark for administrative costs in purchasing?"

Many companies continue to ask this question. I believe the causes of this curiosity are many, and they typically include some or all of the following symptoms:

• The business has an overly large supply base and supplier performance is frequently perceived as poor.

• These suppliers receive purchase orders that perpetuate these relationships, so the purchasing department is seen as the major causal factor.

• The purchasing department generally reports to manufacturing and manufacturing organizations are near-term oriented in terms of costs (i.e., they minimize cost elements and cost drivers in the denominator portion of the profit equation).

• Sales and marketing are chartered to worry about the numerator or top line growth.

A consultant, sniffing at these symptoms, can be very interested in obtaining benchmark data on administrative costs as a basis for proposing how many people his client can terminate as a cost reduction.

The common focus on this example, and many other benchmarking projects is on efficiency. Some common measures are: average dollars spent per buyer, average number of suppliers managed per buyer, average cost of a purchase order, etc.

Is it possible that the effectiveness of how requirements are sourced and how supply is managed is a much more important topic for a benchmarking project—a project that could result in tighter focus on how to improve the numerator of our profit equation? Possibly a means to develop some new strategies to increase top line growth and profitability?

In a past column we cited a Honda success in building cars and motorcycles to world class standards with only 320 direct material suppliers. How large of a supply management organizatrion would your boss allow you to manage 320 suppliers? Ten? Twenty? Thirty? Honda has 800 people, most with engineering expertise. If you consider that they are managing approximately 80% of current and future product costs, it makes sense to deploy resources where they can have a major impact.

Given the situation in most companies today, supply costs greatly exceed manufacturing value added. Core competencies, not headcount reductions, in supply management should be management's long-term objective.

In some situations it might even make sense if manufacturing reports to supply management. An attendee of a workshop I facilitated called recently to advise me of a reorganization her president was making because he agreed with my point. All feeder plants making components for end products will no longer report to manufacturing. Instead, they will report to supply management. In the president's view, this was analogous to a make or buy decision.

Benchmarking, when done well, can lead to dramatic changes in our beliefs, opinions, and mindsets.

Common bad benchmarking practices

Benchmarking continues to thrive in many successful businesses. It should. It's an excellent process to generate continuous improvement. However, given enough time, any managerial tool can become afflicted with local bad practices.

A very common bad practice is that benchmarking projects are not well chosen and defined. A vaguely defined project does not have a high probability of success.

Too often would-be benchmarkers start a project without sufficient definition of critical measures that are appropriate to the specific project undertaken. This requires current knowledge and understanding of internal performance trends to the critical performance measures previously identified.

Members participating as a team in the benchmarking process may not spend enough time developing an appropriate set of questions that will serve to gather the required benchmarking responses from best-practice target companies. Such a questionnaire should have some appeal to potential host companies as a means for them to obtain some benefit from agreeing to your requests for information. If they perceive your project poorly, they will decline your requests for information. Be sure to identify what benefits your benchmarking partner will gain from participating.

Too often, companies put people they can spare on site visit teams. Your best people should visit best-practice companies. This includes managers and directors. They may, after all, be the greatest beneficiaries of insights gained at best-practice sites.

Be sure to focus on processes during site visits and be sure to gather meaningful responses to your questionnaire. Too often site visits can be classified as industrial tourism—everyone has a pleasant time together, but not much of real value is learned.

Too much time during the site visit often is spent discussing information that could have been acquired beforehand. This precludes a more in-depth understanding of how the host company was able to develop its competencies.

Selecting the specific companies that represent best practices is not an easy task. It requires effective research. It's much too easy to target nearby companies. Also, it can be a mistake to restrict a study to one industry. U.S. auto companies would be more successful today if they had been willing to learn from other industries.

The greatest, and all too common, bad practice is failure to implement improvement ideas identified by the benchmarking team. Its report is written and filed away. What a wasted opportunity!

Common benchmarking errors to avoid

Normally, I focus on how to use benchmarking to improve operations. This time, I'll provide guidance on what to avoid doing by illustrating some candidates for "worst practices."

When I first heard the term "benchmarking," it was used in the context of a measured comparison of the operating speeds of competing pieces of computer hardware. I came away thinking that benchmarking was about ratios and comparisons of my company to others, especially if the others were big competitors.

There is a danger, however, in getting caught up with numbers when time might better be spent examining processes. Example: It is important to know the cost of cutting a purchase order when your competitors are using new processes like electronic commerce, integrated supply, resident suppliers, supplier-managed inventory, etc.

Is it important to know the number of suppliers each of your buyers manages? This is only an efficiency measure. A more useful measure is how much value can be created through collaboration between your buyers and suppliers. This is an effectiveness benchmark, which is not easy to calculate, but very valuable.

Too often, purchasing pros believe that benchmarking focuses only on their industry and its key players. A question often asked is "How do the prices we pay compare to the big guys?" Instead, purchasing pros should focus on choosing the best possible benchmarking partner to learn from, regardless of industry, company size, location, etc. Companies like Dell Computer, Wal-Mart,

Chrysler, and Honda of America use best practices that can be applied almost anywhere.

Many senior executives are too busy to benchmark, so they appoint people they can spare on benchmarking projects. But the urgency of dealing with today's problems may not leave time to seek permanent process solutions. And using people that can be spared is not the way; they may not be be capable of discovering best-practice solutions to problems. In some companies, being picked for a benchmarking team, or even being a team leader, are not seen as career-enhancing assignments. And reports from the team usually don't dwell on previous failures by management to adopt best practices.

A common problem is that senior people are too busy to train team members on how to effectively benchmark. A typical refrain is "We must have our report completed in 60 to 90 days, and training and project planning are luxuries we can't afford."

Remembering my earlier computer benchmarking experience was helpful because it made me recall an appropriate truism: "Garbage in, garbage out."

Key negative factors to remember

In looking to strike a balance between benchmarking theory and practice it is often good to sample the opportunities for things to go wrong that can result in an unsuccessful benchmarking project.

An early failure all too often causes an organization to adopt a "been there, done that", mentality that precludes future major opportunities to improve themselves. Hopefully, it's possible to get key points across more effectively by emphasizing what not to do, rather what to do. Borrowing from David Letterman's methodology, here's my list of key benchmarking points to remember:

First, don't worry that project scope, goals, and objectives are clearly understood by all team members. Confusion can easily occur as team members go forth on differing, imcompatible paths.

Second, many teams get staffed with people who are available and that can be spared. Important projects shouldn't be launched without your best, appropriate people as team members. Doing otherwise can frequently lead to more harm than good.

Third, training and education in benchmarking has not been done. The project deadline is tight and doesn't allow time for training. The project manager is inexperienced in process benchmarking.

Fourth, senior executives frequently are too busy to personally direct, participate in, or support process benchmarking in a critical area. Change initiatives that are highly successful invariably have strong top management support that enables barriers to be removed.

Fifth, is a byproduct of inadequate training and education: The methodology used is ineffective. The manifestations are many. A few follow:

• An inexperienced project manager may not communicate very frequently, and effectively.

• Team members place a low priority and value on team participation.

• Meeting attendance is infrequent and spotty as supervisors frequently insist their people work on today's fires in their department.

• Teams too often fail to develop attractive bait to snare the interest of best practice companies they wish to investigate and to understand their reasons for success in a particular area. Why should Dell, Wal-Mart, etc. host your team and answer your questions?

• The project planning of inexperienced teams all too often spends insufficient attention on ensuring their questions can be analyzed accurately. Objectivity is better than subjectivity.

• A team where members don't have clear roles or committee assignments is likely to fail.

• Team members that are drafted don't normally make good soldiers. Competent volunteers are much better.

• Overly broad projects, poorly funded, with a tight deadline are apt to leave a stain in the personnel file of the project leader and team members. An important project must be managed appropriately.

Section 6

WINNING SUPPORT

Bring the mountain to Mohammed...What's in it for me?, Speak a language top management can understand...What top management likes to hear.

Bring the mountain to Mohammed

For several years I have been writing about benchmarking and what I call continuous comparison in the world of supply management. Prior experience leads me to believe that many companies should adopt a strategic, non-adversarial, collobarative approach to supply base management and strategic sourcing.

Typically presidents are very busy people with little time for benchmarking. Often they have a staff chartered for the task. Few subordinates feel secure enough to suggest that if all functions need to apply best practices in achieving benchmark status, the same principle should apply to top management. The problem becomes: How do we get appropriate information delivered to the executives who will benefit from the communication process?

Corporations routinely have important meetings at certain times of the year, firming up strategies and future plans. A small number bring in unbiased experts in applying new ideas, for example, someone with personal credibility in supply management. This can be (and frequently is) an effective way for senior executives to do some continuous comparison. Among the many benefits that can result:

• It can be a significant learning experience for key people who discover new ideas that are proven and applicable to their business.

• Leaders recognize omissions in their strategic plans that should be quickly addressed.

• They learn that their improvement targets are probably too low.

• They note that stretch goals can result in breakthrough thinking and cooperation across functions.

• A common experience across a broad functional audience counteracts potential disbelief from those outside the function.

• A credible expert in this type of event can be a productive outward look and companion against an internally focused culture that is adroit at fending off change.

What's in it for me?

This is a very legitimate question for a busy person to ask about any suggestion perceived to add more work to a lean or downsized organization. Benchmarking cannot be successfully accomplished by eliminating coffee breaks and shortening lunch periods. To benchmark well, it must be a priority. And to make benchmarking a priority in this day and age requires that you de-prioritize some other activities to free up competent resources. This is well worth thinking about over a cup of coffee or a quiet lunch.

For example, lets look at the quality function and see if benchmarking was useful. A few short years ago, the business news pages were filled with articles about the poor quality of U.S.-made products, expanding imports, proliferating factory layoffs, and projections over the demise of yet another U.S. manufacturing company.

Today, we read about a growing number of U.S. manufacturers that are the leaders in their industries and about the barriers other nations erect to prevent the import of our manufactured goods into their countries—Japan included.

U.S. companies began to do things better as part of their renewal process. Senior management leadership was and still is a critical success factor. Benchmarking also was a critical in so far as good and great ideas (best practices) were discovered in use at role-model, successful companies. And quality managers led and caused implementation of good ideas in their processes. Quality has been dramatically improved in many companies. As a result, shareholders are happy and the head of quality has frequently been elevated, properly so, to an executive level.

In many companies today, the logistics function is a proactive leader in benchmarking comparisons as logistics costs have long been an untapped cost reduction opportunity. In some companies logistics costs exceed manufacturing costs (which in recent years have been aggressively reduced, downsized, and outsourced). Today the pace of change is very rapid in logistics and the corporate stature of logistics directors is growing. Logistics managers are frequently part of the strategic planning process in their companies and there is considerable knowledge and re-use from benchmarking studies.

Speak a language top management can understand

Supply management is widely seen as having profound leverage to generate profits. I see it as a rarely and infrequently tapped mine of enormous opportunity. Some of the industry pros I have referred to in past columns believe their activities could yield up to 30% future cost improvements. These pros are the current best-practice leaders who have generated huge cost improvements, and they still can see 30% or more in waste to be eliminated.

A major factor in the past successes of these professionals has been strong, consistent support from CEOs, COOs, CFOs, etc. This support has resulted in diminished creation and perpetuation of waste by the historically powerful functions of engineering, manufacturing, sales, and marketing. So often in the past, these functions have ignored the protestations of their purchasing professionals.

Certainly, support from top management is a critical factor for any change in management processes. And there are countless advocates of change pleading for the support of top management for their new ideas. Personally, however, I have met very few purchasing pros that are able to sell their supply management initiatives. A fair question for a benchmarking project is "How do I sell them.

First, I believe we must cease and desist in using the language of our profession. Indeed, our jargon is not widely understood and does not result in widespread respect and credibility for major strategic contributions.

Second, we must consistently communicate plans, goals, results, etc., in the official language or jargon of top management. Senior management commonly uses terms such as ROI, EPS, market share, dollars rather than things, etc. In essence, all plans, goals, and results, should be translated beforehand into ROI, EPS, etc. This greatly, in my experience, increases the probability of making the sale.

Many companies may be pursuing new systems, such as enterprise resource planning (ERP), as the supply chain solution. Many CEOs have given their CIOs vast sums to spend, and budgets frequently run out long before the complex system is operational. This is an additional reason to do some effective, hands-on benchmarking of successful supply management organizations. Be sure the people you listen to are objective and don't have a booming business in supporting complex system approaches when effective customer-supplier relationships are the critical success factor.

What top management likes to hear

A key first step in winning top management support for the implementation of new processes is to understand the key factors in successful best practice organizations

In prior writings I have referenced Honda of America's best practices and superb results under Dave Nelson, it's head of supply management for 10 years.

In September, 1995, Honda and Dave Nelson received Purchasing Magazine's Medal of Professional Excellence.

More recently Deere and Co. persuaded Dave Nelson to leave Honda and join Deere as its global vice president of supply, a critically important assignment.

Periodically I have stressed the importance of being influential and capable of selling top management to support your plans and strategy to better manage supply.

So what do you think Dave Nelson is telling his management while the manufacturing industry is slowing down? Many of your companies are in the news as they downsize your operations. Deere sales, I believe, are also slowing as farm product exports to Asia are way down.

What would you do if you joined a company and learned you

had just over 1000 people in supply management and approximately 1600 suppliers? Many of you would plan to reduce, significantly, both populations. Is this the best approach for your shareholders?

Some of you would do a Pareto Analysis, and discover approximately 165 suppliers were 70% of the total flow through. Then you might be tempted to really chop the size of both populations. But is this really a better alternative?

Dave Nelson, again, took a different approach. He sold his top management on giving him more resources—$20 million more annually. In return, he promised a ten-fold annual improvement in savings, or an additional $200 million.

This is the kind of best practice—even world-class thinking—that effective benchmarkers gather, analyze, and put in place in their operations. It's also the kind of best practice top management understands and responds to.

Section 7

BENCHMARKERS AND THEIR PARTNERS

How to raise your odds of winnnig a good partner...To whom should we talk?...Where's the chicken?...good conferences lead to good partnering...The benchmarker's code of conduct.

How to raise your odds
of winning a good partner

Last week was spent in discussions with commodity team members seeking advice so they could increase and accelerate benefits from a major supply chain re-engineering project. I inquired about the search for best practices by each team that had not met its economic goals. The responses were few and repetitive: "We ran out of time...We couldn't reach consensus in the team...We didn't know how to approach them..." It's easy to see why the teams had a significant shortfall in effectiveness—they lacked the expertise of succesful practitioners.

But let's focus now on how to get in the door of a high-profile, best-practice company in your area of interest. I recall an instance where a cross-functional team was hard at work on its project to develop design guidelines for packaging materials that dramatically reduced solid wastes and were environmentally friendly. Near the end of the project the team realized that it had made a major error in ignoring benchmarking as an important source of information.

I was asked to do the benchmarking, and to have it done in 2-3 weeks! I first contacted major packaging materials suppliers for leads on customers who might be best-practice firms. I insisted on looking at nominations from the entire spectrum of customers—in this case from premium-priced ice cream manufacturers to large mainframe computer manufacturers. I was able to secure the names, phone, and tax numbers of the people deemed experts in packaging at specific companies of possible relevance to our project.

Next I prepared a benchmarking questionnaire that was designed to gather the specific information the team needed, and the team members approved it.

Then I called the packaging experts at each target company seeking their participation in benchmarking. I specifically told them what they would get in return for their cooperation—a summary report of our findings on the questions they answered. If they answered the entire survey, they would receive a complete report in less than 30 days.

Eleven of the 12 companies I contacted cooperated. Two firms were head and shoulders ahead of the pack. One required us to sign a nondisclosure agreement. The others cooperated beyond our wildest expectations and were of immense help to the team and its project.

As a result, the team was able to quickly develop its design guidelines and was able to identify an initial savings potential of $5 million.

Benchmarking, when approached properly, yields dramatic benefits and can allow your company to interact in a customer network of experts that you have created. Once in, it is up to you to earn your way as a valued contributor and participant.

To whom should we talk?

Whether we call it benchmarking or continuous comparison, the process typically starts with a significant problem and the need for prompt resolution. Where should we look for help?

You may have heard the frequently told tale of a Remington Arms cartridge plant in Arkansas. Management was stumped on how best to solve a customer complaint: Cartridges were neither smooth nor shiny enough. Nearby was a Maybelline plant that produced cosmetics including lipsticks in smooth, shiny cases. A visit to this facility produced the answers.

In this example, a worthy solution was close by. But, if you restrict your search to local sources, you may discover only someone who is "best in class" in Little Rock. Meanwhile, the best solution may be miles away and undiscovered by those who restrict their search.

I started comparing or benchmarking at age 25 when I was suddenly promoted to production and inventory control manager for a leading HVAC manufacturer. The need for benchmarking developed from new responsibilities in areas where I lacked knowledge and experience, and my college training was of no value. Where to look? Automatic Electric, a huge part of GTE, was frequently cited as a leading Chicago-area company. Its production and inventory control manager, Phil Link, was cited also as a functional expert. I phoned Phil, introduced myself, and identified my great interest in learning the secrets of success from a respected professional.

Would you deny such a request? Neither did Phil Link. Over the following years, he kindly hosted me and some associates a number of times in our quest for good answers. Subsequently, Automatic Electric and my employer were both frequently cited by

Chicago-area IBM sales reps as firms at which to study effective production control organizations.

Some years later I repeated the process when I joined my prior employer as corporate director of materials. Having spent my whole career in the real world of local operations, I needed a sense of what processes were relevant in the corporate world. The old line, "Hi, I'm Ken Stork, can I come and learn your secrets of success?" always worked on a peer basis.

Where's the chicken?

When considering benchmarking or continuous comparison in definition of a specific project, it is important to evaluate best in class chicken rather than its egg (output).

The accounts payable process, for instance, is a popular area for reengineering. I receive many calls for advice from individuals with direction from their management to reduce the cost of this nonvalue-added activity—cost reduction equals fewer full-time equivalents (FTEs).

A service center is typically a centralized location for conducting an activity such as accounts payable. I fear that companies seeking a roadmap to an excellent service center are apt to find more eggs and no best in class chicken.

Why? Accounts payable, despite being part of the important finance function, is a downstream output of the supply management or purchasing function. A potentially valuable continuous comparison project should start with with the procurement process and end with accounts payable.

Rather than focus on how many FTEs can be subtracted from the payroll (a focus on efficiency), why not look at the effectiveness of the procurement process? This is much more difficult than a focus on near-term headcount reduction. However, a five, 10, or greater than 25% improvement in actual dollars committed and related ownership costs is possible in many organizations. Benchmark organizations have demonstrated these results historically.

An effective project in this area requires a cross-functional team of purchasing, financial, quality, and technical experts for most companies to discover efectiveness solutions.

A leading example of the supply management process is a company that, as a by-product of strategic sourcing, has eliminated 120,000 invoices. One person lives where 70 employees processed all that paper.

Good conferences lead to good partnering

Educational conferences can be an excellent process for continuous comparison benchmarking. And when the Association for Manufacturing Excellence recently held its annual conference in Boston, many attendees took time to participate in plant tours of leading Boston area companies.

BOSE Corp., famous for its JIT II program, conducted one such tour. Attendees were able to gain an in-depth understanding of JIT II. They learned, for example, what management action prompted Lance Dixon to develop JIT II, what is meant by co-location, what kinds of commodities are involved, and risks that need to be managed. And they received the insights needed to start similar processes in their own firms.

I attended a plant tour of a local Boston area firm, Nypro. The firm is a well known, world class maker of precision, injection molded products. Nypro started in a garage and today has 18 manufacturing plants around the world serving local customers.

Nypro founder and CEO, Gordon Lankton, is a progressive

leader. So much so that I believe he created a new JIT phase, JIT III.

Nypro has intelligently focused considerable attention on its customer base—approximately 30 customers represent 80% (plus) of its annual sales. Its goal is to serve a few good customers exceptionally well so as to prosper from a few unique customer-supplier relationships in growth industries. The automotive industry historically has not been noted for progressive supplier relationships. Nypro does not sell to this industry.

Nypro builds new plants very close to its best customers. Co-location of supplier and customer employees also is practiced here. A new Nypro plant on the West Coast is three miles away from its major customer, Hewlett-Packard. This new plant represents a significant investment to serve a rapidly growing product line. This Nypro facility also contains the customer's product development technical center. In this instance, approximately 20 of the customer's employees are co-located in the supplier's plant.

I came away from Nypro and the conference with a belief that JIT III has been born.

If JIT II makes sense for your company, but you haven't begun implementation, you have another good idea to consider—and implement. Were you a good customer last year. Will your best customers let you co-locate with them?

The benchmarker's code of conduct

Too little time and attention is devoted to the obligations that come with the process of benchmarking another organization. Individuals and organizations must abide by the following principles of ethical conduct:

• **Confidentiality.** Treat a benchmarking interchange as something confidential to the individuals and organizations involved.

Information obtained must not be communicated outside the partnering organizations without prior consent of the participants. An organization's participation in a study should not be communicated externally without permission.

• **Legality.** Avoid discussions of actions that might lead to or imply an interest in restraint of trade: market or customer allocation schemes, price fixing, dealing arrangements, bid rigging, bribery, or misappropriation. Do not discuss costs with competitors if costs are an element of pricing.

• **Exchange.** Be willing to provide the same level of information that you request in any benchmarking exchange.

• **Use.** Information obtained in benchmarking should be used only for the purpose of improvement of operations within the partnering companies themselves. External use or communication of a benchmarking partner's name with its data or observed practices requires permission of that partner. As a consultant or client, do not extend one company's benchmarking study findings to another without the company's permission.

• **Preparation.** Demonstrate commitment to the efficiency and effectiveness of the benchmarking process with adequate preparation at each process step, particularly at initial partnering contact.

• **First-party contact.** Initiate contacts, wherever possible, through a benchmarking contact designated by the partner company. Obtain mutual agreement with the contact on any handoff of communication or responsibility to other parties.

• **Third-party contact.** Obtain an individual's permission before providing his or her name in response to a contact request.

These seven principles comprise a code of conduct that has been adopted by The Strategic Partnering Institute, The International Benchmarking Clearinghouse, The Benchmarking Exchange.

I am highlighting the importance of these seven obligations and principles as I strongly feel they need to be observed universally.

Section 8

MEASUREMENT DRIVES SUCCESS

What's measured gets done...A case for common metrics...Do we ask the right questions and measure what's really important?...Just how good are we?...Why supplier scorecards are critical.

What's measured gets done

Measurements are critical elements to accelerating the rate of change in an organization. Peter Drucker has concluded that few factors are as important as measurement to the performance of an organization. He also noted that measurement is the weakest area in many organizations today.

From my years of personal experience in operations, I have concluded that supply management and other organizations need to reengineer themselves as follows:

• Future success demands that an organization accelerate its rate of change.

• Change requires new behaviors from our employees, suppliers, and customers.

• New behaviors require new and/or revised measurement and rewards systems.

• Trashing obsolete measures is a necessary step toward success.

• Installing and fully using appropriate new measures and rewards greatly accelerates progress toward success.

• Few organizations today are worth benchmarking in this important area.

Primary objectives of measurement are to determine:

• If an organization, function, or process is focused on doing the right things.

• How well it/they are performing.

Primary purposes of performance measurement should be:

• To motivate behavior that leads to continuous improvements in such desired areas as customer satisfaction, quality, flexibility, cost, and productivity.

• To communicate major objectives widely. An excellent example is Motorola's Six Sigma process built on a foundation of common measurement applied widely to all processes.

Current situation that I see in many organizations is:

• Every function, department, or organization has a multitude of charts and graphs that show one or two points that make them look good.

• It is not easy to detect true progress toward the strategic objectives of senior management.

• It is not easy to recognize functions *et al* that are positive or negative contributors to success of the enterprise.

A case for common metrics

Purchasing people frequently complain that they don't get the same respect and clout accorded to other functions, such as finance. A major culprit may be found in purchasing's approach to measurement. That's because a significant attribute of any true profession is wide acceptance and use of a few key common performance measures.

Unfortunately, the purchasing function is notable for an absence of standard commonly accepted measures. If you disagree, ask any 10 buyers for their formula for measuring something as simple as "on-time delivery from suppliers." I guarantee you will get lots of verbiage and multiple responses where management would expect an industry standard to be in place.

Or take "total cost of ownership" and its variants. It has become a common term in our lexicon. Indeed, Lisa Ellram of Arizona State University discovered this term appears in research articles as far back as 1928. Given its long-term popularity in business literature, one would expect researchers to have uncovered successful implementation of a total cost of ownership concept. I haven't read about any, have you? True professions over time do adopt and boldly use good new ideas.

The reengineering dragon continues to gobble up and eliminate many purchasing FTEs (that's consultant-speak for full time equivalents). Frequently the only readily available measure is the cost of the person. Accurate measures of the economic savings that a person or position provided should be in place but are not often readily available.

Some recent studies have shown that in some companies more than 50% of purchases are executed outside the purchasing department. Cost of these procurements would have been less if purchasing people were part of the process. Ironically, these companies are apt to be the ones that are shrinking their purchasing staffs. If common performance measures were in place, that department head might be obtaining management approval to increase staff rather than direction to cut.

The lack of common measures in an organization can be a fatal flaw because it doesn't provide for much real continuous comparison or benchmarking. And when we don't look outside our own organization for knowledge re-use, frequently we don't know what we don't know! Even worse, we may not know that we don't know something that is significant to our business.

Do we ask the right questions and measure what's really important?

Some time back a large airline initiated a review of passenger growth across its entire route structure. As you know, historically this industry has been very cyclical and seasonal. This review was launched during a downturn.

The planners began to revise their schedules and reassigned aircraft from current markets/routes to new routes and to increase service to other current routes. Financial problems persisted and management pressure increased.

The planners made additional schedule revisions. More aircraft were pulled from existing routes and the planners increased further flights to new and other current markets. Financial problems persisted and management pressures increased further.

The planners went back to their task and it resulted in pulling all remaining flights from some old markets and made further increases in service in other markets.

In the end, the airline went out of business. It was overly focused on passenger growth. It failed to look at available capacity on routes where it reduced service. These routes consistently showed low growth because their planes were usually full. The full planes, over time, were directed to other cities where they flew only partially loaded.

Recently I helped a client to install a very important measure—

supplier rating. The suppliers that received the greatest criticism from non-purchasing personnel had nearly perfect performance in the month of July. Favored suppliers of the critics had much poorer performance. The critics retreated and said one month wasn't a representative period. The company now has additional objective supplier rating data on its five most important purchased commodities. The most criticized suppliers are consistently top performers. Those most favored by non-purchasing personnel are consistently poorer performers. I see this scenario frequently, which is why I am a strong advocate of supplier rating/scorecards.

Purchasing organizations that lack objective, consistent, credible measures of supplier performance are vulnerable to other organizations having majority influence in official sourcing selections. It becomes very costly dealing with poor performing suppliers, and if you lack the measures you are doomed to a life of putting out fires started by someone else.

Just how good are we?

Measuring customer satisfaction has been a useful and popular thing to do in recent times. Companies frequently have learned that they aren't nearly as good as they thought. For example, many company managers were very pleased with internal measures of quality for their products and services, for example, timeliness of delivery, service, responsiveness, etc. Then, actual voice-of-the-customer information was gathered and the executives were frequently dismayed that their internal data fell far short of meeting actual customer needs and expectations.

Advancement of concepts like the virtual enterprise can lead to a mindset that excellent suppliers deserve to be treated with the same importance as major customers. If you support this concept, then how well are you doing in meeting the needs, wants, and expectations of your few, but critical suppliers.

If you don't know, but aren't afraid to ask, then you should think about conducting a formal voice-of-the-supplier survey. If you really like the idea, then you should think even longer about how this can be part of your ongoing measurement process so you can periodically can take a reading and plot progress toward a goal that you and your management have established.

Some best practice companies are consistently successful in competitive industries due in part to a strategic approach to supply management. Often they and their major competitors have many common suppliers. But the winners enjoy considerably better support that contributes significantly to their mutual success. The industry followers typically do not see supply relationships as a critical success factor. The thought of measuring supplier satisfaction is a foreign notion to them.

Concepts of identifying and working on achieving shared expectations is an even less common thrust—but one worth considering.

You probably will need an independent third party to conduct an anonymous survey on your behalf.

Today it is still difficult for suppliers to tell the customer directly that he has not been wearing clothes lately. Are you and your company walking the talk with suppliers?

Why supplier scorecards are critical

If your company lacks a credible, effective process to measure performance of key suppliers in a timely fashion, then I doubt your company is effectively managing its supplier relationships. If you're not reporting on supplier performance, key suppliers are likely to give more attention and better performance to customers (possibly your competitors) that are tracking and reporting their performance effectively.

Two of my favorite four-letter words are goal and plan. Most companies have a goal of effectively managing supply and most have a plan for doing so. But goals and plans that lack credible measurement processes are simply statements of good intentions.

Some years ago we implemented a common supplier scorecard in a large global diversified company. We had a multitude of problems and an infinite number of active suppliers. We developed an approach that created an approximation of total cost, allowing high-performing suppliers to sell at higher unit prices. It was a novel idea then, and remains so today. We also widely communicated the process and formula for measuring. We said the best performers would double their market share, and the poorest performers would lose 100% of their business. In a few years this scorecard process yielded incredible, real progress. It created a small, loyal, high-performance supply base that gave us preferential treatment. Because they understood the process, supplier executives could measure their own performance faster than we could publish their scores. Result: We had suppliers taking corrective actions even before we asked.

When it comes to supplier scorecards, there are three key words: credible, effective, and timely.

Credible means the data measured is objective, not subjective. Subjectivity is too often inconsistent or illogical in the eyes of the organization being measured.

Effective means measuring the few things that are high on the customer's priority lists. Hundreds of times I have asked operations executives what should be measured in a supplier scorecard. Always the same responses: delivery and quality. If you don't have a scorecard, start with these first. When delivery and quality issues go away, then you can determine new priorities for measuring and setting goals with suppliers.

Timely means soon after the measurement period ends. Weekly is excellent for high-volume relationships; daily is desirable in a relationship using EDI. Monthly should be the maximum. Infrequent distribution of supplier scorecards implies that they aren't important.

Performance measurement is rarely a strength of an organization. This is all too true for purchasing operations trying to manage supply. Supplier scorecards should be a high priority.

Index

A quick reference to topics covered in Benchmarking: In Theory and Practice

A

B

D

Definitions of benchmarking, 14-16

Delay & complexity, need to minimize, 72

Design for procurement, 172

Differentiation, value of, 161-162

E

Early success, the imporance of, 71

Education and training for benchmarking, 162-163

F

Finding benchmarking partners, 93-102

  Asking the right questions, 96, 97

  Overcoming obstacles, 94-95

  What sells benchmarking partners, 93-94

Ford and the need to ask the right questions, 35-37

Ford's River Rouge as an inspiration for benchmarking, 24-25

Functional evaluations, 44

Funding, the minimum needed, 74

Functional lines, the need to cross them, 46

Functional peer reviews, 164-166

G

GE and benchmarking mindset, 130-131
GE and comparative analysis, 23
Generator of ideas, a prime benchmarking use, 55-56

H

Help, some thoughts on winning it, 207-208
Honda purchasing headcount, 173
Host approval, planning for, 77-78
How benchmarking sometimes gets a bad name, 119
Humility can pay off, 60-61

I

Identifying opportunities for benchmarking, 27
Importance of benchmarking, 21-27
Improvement model, chart, 122
Information sharing, limits on, 179-180
Industry Week's 10 best plants awards, 126
Insourcing, benchmark it!, 123-124
Integration stage, 42, 156-158

M

Machiavelli, Niccolo, on change, 99
Materials management, what went wrong, 148-149
Maturation, how benchmarking is growing up, 131-132
Mazda's accounts payables, 36-37
Measuring results, 105-115, 215-216
  Case for common metrics, 216-218
  Chrysler's SCORE program, 109-110
  Do we measure the right things?, 218-219
  Driving behavior, 107-108
  Logic of good measurements, chart, 115
  Measurement essentials, what companies need to measure, 111-113
  Measures needed to drive change, 106-107
  What about customer satisfaction?, 219-220
  What measurements are needed, 110-111
Measurements linked to strategic plan and key beliefs, chart, 114
Mindset, how a benchmarking one pays off, 130-131
Multi-level thinking, 60

N

Nelson, Dave, 173-174, 188-189, 201-202
Networking, a key quality for project leaders, 49
Numbers, the danger of, 75-76,161

O

Old mindsets that can hinder success, 187-189

Outsourcing sourcing, 129-130

P

Partners, shortage of suitable ones, 85-86

Partners, raising the odds of winning a good one, 205-207

Performance measurements, purpose of, 115

Pitfalls to avoid, 71-79

Planning a benchmarking effort, 153-154

Porter, Michael E., on change, 99

Preparing for a benchmarking project, 72-73

Product introduction and benchmarking, 33-34

Process benchmarking

  Defining the key processes, 45

  Understanding the key processes, 46-48

Projects, finding a suitable first project, 49-50

Purchasing departments, how they compare, 169

Q

Questionnaires, 206

Questionnaires, importance of, 78